The Grace Awakening
Workbook

Books for Adults

Active Spirituality
Bedside Blessings
Behold . . . The Man!
The Bride
Come Before Winter
Compassion: Showing We Care in a Careless World
The Darkness and the Dawn
Day by Day
Dear Graduate
Dropping Your Guard
Elijah: A Man of Heroism and Humility
Encourage Me
Esther: A Woman of Strength and Dignity
The Finishing Touch
Flying Closer to the Flame
For Those Who Hurt
God's Provision
The Grace Awakening
Growing Deep in the Christian Life
Growing Strong in the Seasons of Life
Growing Wise in Family Life
Hand Me Another Brick
Home: Where Life Makes Up Its Mind
Hope Again
Improving Your Serve
Intimacy with the Almighty
Job: A Man of Heroic Endurance
Job: Interactive Study Guide
Joseph: A Man of Integrity and Forgiveness

Killing Giants, Pulling Thorns
Laugh Again
Leadership: Influence That Inspires
Living Above the Level of Mediocrity
Living Beyond the Daily Grind, Books I and II
The Living Insights Study Bible—General Editor
Living on the Ragged Edge
Make Up Your Mind
Man to Man
Moses: A Man of Selfless Dedication
The Mystery of God's Will
Paul: A Man of Grit and Grace
The Quest for Character
Recovery: When Healing Takes Time
The Road to Armageddon
Sanctity of Life
Simple Trust
Starting Over
Start Where You Are
Strengthening Your Grip
Stress Fractures
Strike the Original Match
The Strong Family
Suddenly One Morning
The Tale of the Tardy Oxcart
Three Steps Forward, Two Steps Back
Victory: A Winning Game Plan for Life
Why, God?
You and Your Child

Minibooks

Abraham: A Model of Pioneer Faith
David: A Model of Pioneer Courage
Esther: A Model of Pioneer Independence

Moses: A Model of Pioneer Vision
Nehemiah: A Model of Pioneer Determination

Booklets

Anger
Attitudes
Commitment
Dealing with Defiance
Demonism
Destiny
Divorce
Eternal Security
Forgiving and Forgetting
Fun Is Contagious!
God's Will
Hope
Impossibilities
Integrity
Intimacy with the Almighty
Leisure
The Lonely Whine of the Top Dog

Make Your Dream Come True
Making the Weak Family Strong
Moral Purity
Our Mediator
Peace . . . in Spite of Panic
Portrait of a Faithful Father
The Power of a Promise
Prayer
Reflections from the Heart—A Prayer Journal
Seeking the Shepherd's Heart—A Prayer Journal
Sensuality
Stress
This is No Time for Wimps
Tongues
When Your Comfort Zone Gets the Squeeze
Woman

Books for Children

Paw Paw Chuck's Big Ideas in the Bible

The Grace Awakening Workbook

BASED ON THE BOOK BY
CHARLES R. SWINDOLL

Produced in association with CREATIVE MINISTRIES
Insight for Living

W PUBLISHING GROUP™
www.wpublishinggroup.com

A Division of Thomas Nelson, Inc.
www.ThomasNelson.com

THE GRACE *Awakening* WORKBOOK

By Charles R. Swindoll

Published by W Publishing Group, A Division of Thomas Nelson, Inc., P. O. Box 141000, Nashville, Tennessee, 37214.

ISBN 0-8499-4531-3

Printed in the United States of America
03 04 05 06 VG 9 8 7 6 5 4 3 2 1

The Grace Awakening Workbook

Charles R. Swindoll has devoted his life to the clear, practical teaching and application of God's Word and His grace. A pastor at heart, Chuck has served as senior pastor to congregations in Texas, Massachusetts, and California. He currently pastors Stonebriar Community Church in Frisco, Texas, but Chuck's listening audience extends far beyond a local church body. As a leading program in Christian broadcasting, *Insight for Living* airs in major Christian radio markets around the world, reaching churched and un-churched people groups in languages they can understand. Chuck's extensive writing ministry has also served the body of Christ worldwide, and his leadership as president and now chancellor of Dallas Theological Seminary has helped prepare and equip a new generation for ministry. Chuck and Cynthia, his partner in life and ministry, have four grown children and ten grandchildren.

Based on the original outlines, charts, and transcripts of Charles R. Swindoll's sermons, the workbook text was developed and written by Suzanne Keffer, Th.M., Dallas Theological Seminary, and Michael J. Svigel, Th.M., Dallas Theological Seminary. Contextual support material was provided by the creative ministries department of Insight for Living.

Editor in Chief: Cynthia Swindoll

Director: Brian Goins

Editors: Greg Smith, Amy Snedaker, Marla Alupoaicei

CONTENTS

A Letter from Chuck   ix

How to Use The Grace Awakening Workbook   xi

Chapter 1   1
Grace: It's Really Amazing!

Chapter 2   13
The Free Gift

Chapter 3   25
Isn't Grace Risky?

Chapter 4   37
Undeserving, Yet Unconditionally Loved

Chapter 5   49
Squaring Off against Legalism

Chapter 6   61
Emancipated? Then Live Like It!

Chapter 7   73
Guiding Others to Freedom

Chapter 8   85
The Grace to Let Others Be

Chapter 9   97
Graciously Disagreeing and Pressing On

Chapter 10   109
Grace: Up Close and Personal

Chapter 11   119
Are You Really a Minister of Grace?

Chapter 12   133
A Marriage Oiled by Grace

Chapter 13   145
The Charming Joy of Grace Giving

Chapter 14   155
Grace: It's Really Accepting!

Endnotes   167

Books for Probing Further   175

A Letter from Chuck

BACK IN THE 1700S, a series of revivals in the American colonies led to an awakening. The movement began in the middle colonies and soon spread up north into New England and, shortly thereafter, down south into the Carolinas and Georgia.

Strong-hearted men like Jonathan Edwards, George Whitefield, Gilbert Tennent, and the Wesley brothers delivered powerful messages of the cross, stirring the hearts of thousands. This sweeping movement came to be known as "The Great Awakening." What remarkable changes occurred as a result of God's working!

None can deny that there is the need for yet another awakening among God's people . . . a renewed appreciation for and acceptance of His grace. Grace—the eternal freedom God offers every person through Jesus His Son. When the One who was fully God came to our world in the form of a man and died for our sins, He released all who would believe in Him from the bondage of sin and offered them an undeserved place at His Father's table for eternity. Where sin abounded, grace super-abounded!

When we stop relying on our own strength to please God and choose instead to rely on Jesus's sacrifice on the cross to give us right standing before Him, we become sons and daughters of God and heirs to eternal life. But, ironically, many of us still live our lives as if we are spiritual orphans. Instead of resting in the fact that God loves us fully, we strive to earn his love by doing all the "right" things. Sometimes, we go so far as imposing our "Ways to Earn God's Approval" list on others. It's time for us to stop denying grace to ourselves and each other and start embracing its freedom.

What is it that causes our Lord to stoop and reach out to us in love? Grace. What is it that frees us to be all He means us to be? Grace. What is it that permits others to be who they are . . . sometimes very different from us? Grace. What adds oil to the friction points of a marriage, freeing both partners from pettiness and negativism? Grace. And what gives magnetic charm to a ministry, inviting others to become a part? Again, as always . . . grace.

Hopefully, as you work your way through the following pages, new dimensions of grace will become a reality to you. Since God is still working today as He did many years ago, you may very well experience your own personal awakening of grace.

Chuck Swindoll

How to Use
The Grace *Awakening* Workbook

W E HOPE THIS WORKBOOK from our Insights and Application line of biblical resources will help you to fully embrace grace—letting the liberty it brings free you from the pressure we often feel to perform for God's approval. Use this workbook as a tool in your personal devotions, small-group studies, or church curriculum.

Personal Devotions—When your one-on-one time with God needs direction, this workbook will guide you on the path toward greater wisdom, knowledge, and spiritual maturity.

Small-Group Bible Studies—When your small group desires to lay biblical foundations and build authentic community, this workbook provides you with a blueprint for learning God's Word and for encouraging each other as you live together under His construction.

Church Curriculum—When your church body needs a resource that offers real answers to tough questions, this workbook offers biblical truth, straight answers, and life-application questions in an exciting, conversation-stimulating format.

Every workbook chapter contains two regular features:

Soaring on His Word encourages you to memorize Scripture that will help you live by grace.

Spreading Your Wings challenges you to put grace into action in your everyday life.

Some workbook chapters contain one or more of the following special features:

 Flying Against the Winds of Our Culture asks you to consider the "countergrace" messages our world sends and how these ideas distort our understanding of true grace.

 Getting to the Root lets you tap into the original meanings of Hebrew and Greek words from the original text.

 Digging Deeper offers you the opportunity to gain deeper insight into specific aspects of Christian theology addressed in the chapters.

 *Windows to the Ancient World* takes you back in time to experience the history, culture, and customs of the biblical world.

May His grace enable you to loosen your grip on the "I should" and open your hands to the "He will."

1
GRACE: IT'S REALLY AMAZING!

 Soaring on His Word

And the Word became flesh, and dwelt among us, and we saw His glory, glory as of the only begotten from the Father, full of grace and truth.

— JOHN 1:14

*E*RNIE INCHED ON HIS BELLY through the dirt. When the Great Monarch had called him to become a butterfly, He had promised warmth. He spoke of awakening to freedom. But since his cocooned transformation, Ernie had tired under the load of his wings. The Great Monarch had said his wings would carry him through the journey, but Ernie considered them a heavy and cumbersome burden. He tried tucking them to the left, shifting them to the right, and folding them together. But nothing reduced the drag of their dead weight.

This morning's gales blew so hard against his delicate flaps that Ernie toppled twice. At this rate, he would never make it south of the border in time. But he had to keep crawling. Even if he wasn't gaining much ground, this was the only way to Mexico.

No sign of his missing comrades. Where were they? Had they gotten lost? Swoosh! Swoosh! Swoosh! What was that strange sound?

Swoosh! Swoosh! Swoosh! Ernie froze—hoping not to be seen.

Orange and black fliers filled the sky, gliding effortlessly on the wind. What could these fancy flutterers want with him?

As one flutterer hovered overhead, he questioned, "What in the world are you doing down there?"

Ernie called back, "I'm making my way to winter in Mexico. I'm a peaceful butterfly. I don't want any trouble."

"You're a what?"

"A butterfly. I used to be a caterpillar, but that was before the Great Monarch called me to follow Him. When I joined Him, he transformed me from a caterpillar to a butterfly. He gave me my wings."

"Oh you poor caterfly!"

"I didn't say caterfly. I said butterfly: B-U-T-T-E-R-F—"

"Nope. You're definitely a caterfly—the wing-crawling gives you away."

"Wing-crawling?"

"Yep. Caterflies know the Great Monarch has given them wings, but they don't use them as the Great Monarch intended. They're still trying to crawl on the ground against the wind rather than letting their wings carry them *on* the wind."

"On the wind?"

"On the wind. You're a butterfly. Stop inching around in the dirt like a caterpillar! Use your wings. Fly!"

Ernie tentatively drew his wings together and then spread them wide apart. Together. Apart. Together. Apart. Together . . . *swoosh!*

The wings Ernie had considered a burden now carried him on the wind. Swooshing and gliding with his comrades, Ernie finally understood that the Great Monarch had given him wings so that he could soar.

Just as the Great Monarch gave Ernie wings, God offers us grace through His Son, Jesus. When it comes to how much we rely on His grace, we're all caterpillars, butterflies, or caterflies.

Caterpillars are people who have never said yes to God's invitation to receive His gift of eternal life and be transformed from the inside out. They've never accepted Jesus's sacrifice on the cross as full payment for their sins. They've never established a true relationship with God through His Son. Instead, they continue to inch through the dirt, futilely trying to make life work apart from the One who created them and gives meaning to life.

Butterflies are people who used to be caterpillars, but God has radically changed them. They have trusted in Christ's death as payment for their sins, have established a relationship with God by faith, and have received His life within them. God has given them a new heart that knows Him and wants to follow Him. They live in the freedom of God's grace, knowing that the pressure is off because of what Christ has done for them. Their former emptiness has been filled by the love of God.

Caterflies are butterflies who have been radically changed on the inside but continue to crawl in the dirt, living as if they need to make life work on their own. They haven't learned to fly on the wings of God's grace. Caterflies are still trying to earn God's acceptance through their own strenuous efforts, rather than letting God's grace carry them into freedom, joy, and real life.

Once we accept God's grace and become butterflies, we'll never be caterpillars again. We have left our old selves behind. But all butterflies have some caterfly tendencies. We all find it tempting to fall back on our own strength—crawling on our own—rather than flying free on the wings of grace.

What about you? Are you an untransformed caterpillar, a soaring butterfly, or a wing-crawling caterfly? Explain.

_____

_____

_____

_____

You may not be sure what you are. You may not know if you've ever truly established a relationship with God and been transformed on the inside. Whether you're a caterpillar who's curious about flying on the wings of grace, a butterfly who needs to strengthen your wing skills, or a consistent caterfly who relies on your feet more than your wings, consider this study your enrollment into flight school. It's time for a course in Flying 101.

HAS A GRACE KILLER CLIPPED YOUR WINGS?

If you struggle to fly free on the wings of grace, it may be that a grace killer has clipped your wings. Let's take a closer look at these sometimes well-meaning—but nevertheless destructive—opponents of God's grace.

What's a grace killer? At first glance, grace killers hardly look threatening. They often carry Bibles, lead ministries, and sing in the choir. But their small view of God keeps them chained to rules and regulations they think will keep them and you in right standing with Him. Grace killers use shame, fear, and intimidation to drive themselves and others to please God. Though their mouths say yes to God's offer of forgiveness through His Son, their faces glower no to the freedom in life that Christ brings. When the "no" faces frown at us, our countenances can fall, our creativity can crumble, and our joy can fade.

DIGGING DEEPER

The Pharisees in Jesus's day bring up the important issue of hypocrisy—believing one thing, but living another. Hypocrisy isn't just a practical issue—it is profoundly theological. Like many conservative Christians today, the Pharisees were the "orthodox" folks who held fast to the fundamental truths of Judaism when other parties were trading in the great doctrines of Scripture for liberal philosophy or political agendas (Acts 23:6–8). However, though they were right in much of their theology, they were wrong in their application. Being extremely zealous for the "facts" of the faith, their hearts were not transformed by the faith.

This type of hypocrisy is a real threat even to true Christians, and the New Testament warns against it vigorously (Romans 12:9; James 3:17; 1 Peter 2:1). Head knowledge without heart transformation is just as real a threat today as it was in Jesus's and Paul's day. There is likely no greater menace to the testimony of a Christian than hypocrisy, and we must escape its vile grip.

Jesus had more than a few run-ins with grace killers. In fact, it seemed that grace killers dogged His every step. In Jesus's day, the primary grace killers were a leading religious group known as Pharisees. Just like any religious system that leaves in human hands the task of righting wrong, the Pharisees' system exalted self-sufficiency over God-dependency. Like many people today, these grace killers were obsessed with the Law. Obeying its exact commands was a compulsion. They desperately needed Someone to set them free. See "Windows to the Ancient World" on page 5.

Sometimes we aren't even aware that we are still trying to gain acceptance from God through our own efforts. As an indicator, answer this question: Do you feel more accepted by God when you do the following things (or less accepted when you don't do them)? Check which ones apply.

❏ Read or study your Bible   ❏ Fellowship with other believers

❏ Memorize Scripture   ❏ Avoid certain persistent sins

❏ Pray regularly   ❏ Avoid situations that might not glorify God

❏ Go to church regularly   ❏ Grow in good character qualities

If you checked any of the boxes above, how does it make you feel when you try to keep these rules to gain God's acceptance?

_____

_____

_____

_____

While many of these may be legitimate and worthwhile endeavors, if we do them to gain God's favor, we embrace a performance-based love, which is the opposite of grace.

WINDOWS TO THE ANCIENT WORLD

The following excerpt from the Talmud (a written collection of Judaism's oral traditions) concerning a man who is overtaken by dusk on the eve of the Sabbath reflects the measures the Pharisees took to use the Law as a ladder to reach God rather than recognizing it as a spotlight that revealed their sins.

Mishnah: Should darkness fall upon a person on a road, he entrusts his purse to a Gentile, but if there is no Gentile with him, he places it on the (donkey). When he reaches the outmost courtyard, he removes the object which may be handled on the Sabbath, whilst as for those which may not be handled on the Sabbath, he unties the cords and the sacks fall off automatically.[1]

If you try to keep the rules to gain God's favor, do you think that God will still accept you when you fail to keep the rules?

_____

_____

_____

_____

According to Hebrews 4:14–15 and 10:12–14, does God's acceptance of you really depend on your performance in any of these areas? On whose performance does it depend? How well did He perform on your behalf?

_____

_____

_____

_____

THE FACE OF GRACE

Freedom came when God's Son, Jesus, entered the world as a man (John 1:14). In a time filled with "no"-faced religious leaders, Jesus wore a "yes" face. When Jesus lived among them, the disciples saw one gracious act piled upon another. They saw His glory. They walked alongside the perfect embodiment of grace and truth. Into a culture parched by "Thou shalt nots," the man named "God with us" poured out love and modeled forgiveness and relationship rather than religious obligation (John 1:16–17). His grace overflowed, leaving His disciples filled with a selfless love that freed them and sent a tidal wave of change throughout the Roman world.

THE CASE FOR GRACE

Grace Explained

But what exactly is grace? Is it something that only Jesus possessed?

While the Bible doesn't give us a dictionary-style definition of grace, both the Old and New Testaments overflow with stories of it. Contrary to what many people think, God showered it upon the Old Testament people who followed Him.

To understand the full meaning of grace, we need to return to the Hebrew word *chen*, meaning "to bend or stoop." Over time, the term came to include the idea of "condescending favor." Grace is the kind of favor a peasant girl feels when the queen kneels and touches her head. The kind of favor a criminal receives when the president pardons him. Neither the child nor the criminal has done anything to earn it. Yet, the queen and the president choose to bestow it out of the goodness of their hearts.

When "grace and truth were realized through Jesus Christ," a long-awaited revolution of the heart began to set religious captives free. Fearful bondage motivated by guilt was replaced with a fresh motivation to follow Him in truth simply out of a deep devotion and delight. Rather than focusing on the accomplishments of the flesh, He spoke of the heart. Instead of demanding that the sinner fulfill a long list of requirements, He emphasized faith, if only the size of a mustard seed.
—The Grace Awakening

Love that goes upward is adoration; love that goes outward is affection; love that stoops is grace.[2]
—Donald Grey Barnhouse

Snapshots of grace fill the pages of the Old Testament. Take a moment to refresh your memory or to look up these great moments that showcase grace.

> Joseph's showering the brothers who sold him into slavery with grain, land, and a renewed relationship.
> (Genesis 45)

> God's delivering His grumbling people (who strayed from Him often) out of Egypt and into the Promised Land.
> (Exodus 12; Joshua 3)

> David's restraint not to kill Saul—the man who hated him, hunted him, and hungered for his destruction—when he had the chance.
> (1 Samuel 24; 26)

> God's choice to send Jonah to Ninevah, giving a godless people the opportunity to turn to Him.
> (Jonah 1; 3)

Grace is favor extended fully and freely to those who don't deserve it. It's unmerited and unearned. It's firm, persistent, and steadfast.

GRACE EMBODIED

The ultimate New Testament picture of grace is Christ Himself. He literally embodied grace, bestowing favor on those who didn't deserve or earn it.

Read John 8:3–11. How did Jesus's response turn the Pharisees from judging the adulterous woman to examining their own hearts?

_____

_____

_____

_____

Read Luke 23:33–35. How did Jesus demonstrate grace to those who mocked and killed him?

_____

_____

_____

_____

FLYING AGAINST THE WINDS OF OUR CULTURE

Picture this. You're clearing the table after a rushed Monday morning breakfast. Just as you round the corner to collect the last sticky plate, you catch your five-year-old leaving two quarters on the table. "Does this cover my share of the pancakes, Mom? I'm saving the rest of my allowance to pay Dad for driving me to kindergarten."

The contents of Junior's piggy bank could never cover the cost you incur while raising him. And even if he could one day pay you back, you wouldn't want him to. You wash his favorite T-shirt, cut the crusts off of his PB&J sandwiches, and taxi him to T-ball out of love—not out of obligation.

Just as you'd likely feel insulted if your family and friends tried to repay you for your love, our heavenly Father feels insulted when we try to pay Him back for His grace. When grace appears in Scripture, the recipient never deserves it! When we come as sinners before God, we come with nothing to commend us before Him. God accepts us into His family, not because *we deserve* to be His sons and daughters, but because *He desires* us to be His children.

That's grace!

GRACE EMBRACED

The One we could call "Grace Embodied" never tires of extending it to us. When we fully embrace His gift of grace, we will

 have a greater appreciation of God's gifts.

 spend less time and energy concerned about others' choices.

 become more tolerant and joyful, less prejudiced and judgmental.

 take a giant step toward maturity.

Grace will bring the freedom to want the highest good for and expect the highest good from one another. It will make us want to obey and prompt us to love each other. However, when we don't embrace grace for ourselves, we have no grace to offer others.

If we refuse to live by grace, our attitudes sour. We're certain that people can't be trusted. We waver over whether or not God fully accepts us, so we run from intimacy with Him. On our own, we drive ourselves to obsessive intensity. Our spirits harden. Our rigidity repels. Our faces shout, "No!"

When we choose to live by grace, our attitudes shift from negative to positive. Our relationships with people are characterized by confident acceptance rather than suspicious intolerance. With His grace, our entire focus expands. Our intensity is relieved. Our spirits soften. We become more winsome, affirming, contagious, and understanding. Our faces say, "Yes."

Don't frown like a Pharisee. Don't refuse His offer of grace and eternal life in heaven. Don't ignore the grace He gives you to live in freedom while you're on earth. Don't miss an opportunity to extend His grace to those He puts in your path. The grace they see in you will draw them to Him.

Spreading Your Wings

It's impossible to truly offer grace to others and experience all the joys it brings if we have not first accepted grace from God. Think back to the question asked at the beginning of the chapter. Did you classify yourself as a caterpillar, butterfly, or caterfly? Or were you unsure? Let's explore what the Bible has to say about God's gift of eternal life. Jesus says in the Gospel of John: "For God so loved the world that He gave His only begotten Son, that whoever believes in Him shall not perish, but have eternal life" (John 3:16).

According to this verse, how does someone receive eternal life?

_____

_____

_____

_____

_____

_____

_____

This believing in Jesus means receiving Christ Himself into our lives: "But as many as received Him, to them He gave the right to become children of God, even to those who believe in His name" (John 1:12).

There is nothing we can do to earn this salvation. We can only receive it by faith as a free gift. The apostle Paul wrote: "For the wages of sin is death, but the free gift of God is eternal life in Christ Jesus our Lord" (Romans 6:23).

If you desire to have a relationship with God, use the lines below to express your desire to Him.

_____

_____

_____

_____

_____

_____

If you're a butterfly who has already trusted in Christ, do you ever struggle with wing-crawling? In what areas of life do you tend to wing-crawl rather than fly free? How can you embrace His grace more fully in these areas of your life?

_____

_____

_____

_____

_____

_____

If only you had recognized the grace of God
through Jesus Christ our Lord!
If only you had been able to see his incarnation,
in which he took a human soul and body,
as the supreme instance of grace! [3]

—AUGUSTINE

2

THE FREE GIFT

 Soaring on His Word

For by grace you have been saved through faith; and that not of yourselves, it is the gift of God; not as a result of works, so that no one may boast.

—EPHESIANS 2:8–9

HERESY—the word should make every believer bristle. When we hear messages that are contrary to what the Bible says is true, we should sound the alarm. Peter warned us to beware, saying, "There will also be false teachers among you who will secretly introduce destructive heresies . . . bringing swift destruction upon themselves" (2 Peter 2:1). He knew that false teachers' words would entice us to exalt man's misguided messages over God's truth. But the problem is that we're often caught unawares. While many of us consider ourselves savvy to Satan's truth-twisting, the subtle shifts in our culture's thinking can easily ambush us. The latest worldly wisdom sounds so innocuous, we're often unknowingly infected by its insidious lies.

One of today's most dangerous heresies doesn't sound heretical at all. In fact, it rings of solid work ethic and self-made success. Most of us would be proud to wear its stripes of achievement on our sleeves. What is this heresy dressed in honor's clothing? It's humanism—the idea that man is master of his own fate, king of his destiny, captain of his own soul.

William Ernest Henley of Gloucester, England, captured humanism's exaltation of man in his early twentieth-century poem "Invictus."

INVICTUS

Out of the night that covers me,
    Black as the Pit from pole to pole,
I thank whatever gods may be
    For my unconquerable soul.

In the fell clutch of circumstance
    I have not winced nor cried aloud.
Under the bludgeonings of chance
    My head is bloody, but unbowed.

Beyond this place of wrath and tears
    Looms but the Horror of the shade,
And yet the menace of the years
    Finds and shall find me unafraid.

It matters not how strait the gate,
    How charged with punishments the scroll,
I am the master of my fate;
    I am the captain of my soul.[1]

At first blush, these words might seem bold and invigorating. Stalwart and unbending, they seem to march us onward to be something bigger and better than we are, unconquerable souls even! They suggest that, if we dig deep enough, hold on tight enough, and stand tall enough, we'll prevail. So what's wrong with that? They give *us* credit for overcoming rather than acknowledging the One who overcomes for us. It's great to take pride in who you are and to be the best you can be, but to forget God—something's terribly wrong with that philosophy!

These ideas are all around us, championing unconquerable strength of the created over the infinite power of the Creator. Many times we do not even notice small shifts in our worldview. But when we find ourselves trusting our own strength over God's power, following our own desires rather than His direction, or lifting up our success instead of exalting Him for what He does through us, we can be sure that humanism is creeping in.

FLYING AGAINST THE WINDS OF OUR CULTURE

Our modern-day world is filled with mantras similar to those in "Invictus," which extol the virtues of self-sufficient success. Our brightest academicians herald its worth in the halls of higher learning. Our leaders lift its merit in their political speeches. Our artists extol its virtue in poems, songs, books, and screenplays. Consider the words of Frank Sinatra's 1967 hit song "My Way."

MY WAY

And now, the end is near;
And so I face the final curtain.
My friend, I'll say it clear,
I'll state my case, of which I'm certain.

I've lived a life that's full.
I've traveled each and ev'ry highway;
But more, much more than this,
I did it my way. . . .

For what is man, what has he got?
If not himself, then he has not
To say the things he truly feels,
And not the words of one who kneels.
The record shows I took the blows—
And did it my way![2]

"For what is man, what has he got? If not himself, then he has not . . ."—Really? Man doesn't have to kneel to *anyone*?

WARNING: HERESY ON THE LOOSE

When we allow what we do to eclipse what God does for us, we become self-made survivors who think we can weather life's storms with a stronger sense of self and an unbending will. We feed our flesh on pride and starve our souls of God. By the time we realize that apart from God we are famished souls navigating through life in leaky vessels, we find ourselves desperately bailing water from the ship of self we were sure could never sink.

We're not the first to believe that we can master life without the Master's help. Long before Henley penned "Invictus" or Sinatra crooned, "My Way," the early inhabitants of this earth, who lived in a place called Shinar, tried to build their own future by erecting a tower that would exalt their name and their creation over God's name and God's creation. We call it the Tower of Babel. Let's take a moment to travel back to the days of Genesis 11.

Read Genesis 11:1–9. What do you think motivated the people of Shinar to build a city? What verses support your answer?

_____

_____

_____

_____

How would being scattered force the people to rely on God rather than trust in their own strength?

_____

_____

_____

_____

Don't miss what God did at Babel. Notice that He never destroyed the tower. He left it standing permanently under construction to declare His ways greater than man's plans.

It's likely that the people of Shinar, like many of us, thought doing what they wanted to do would result in being what they thought they ought to be. Can't you just see the wheels turning in the head engineer's and the builders' minds: "By building a great tower, we'll make our name known. We'll be famous for years to come." And God steps in and says, "No way! No way will you honor the works of your hands over My creation. No way will you make your name known while ignoring Mine. No way will you make the mistake of thinking that your plans can outdo My ways."

Though mixing up a civilization's language and scattering its people over the earth may seem like a harsh judgment, God acted out of a desire to draw the people back to a knowledge of Him. In the same way, when we forget God and exalt ourselves, He may chasten us severely. But His discipline is always designed to bring us back to Him.

"Wait a minute," you might say. "The people of Shinar were just working hard to reach God, and everyone knows that 'God helps those who help themselves,' right?" Beware of this heresy that sounds so honorable but is truly prideful. This popular, unbiblical grace killer stalks us and ensnares us by convincing us that our efforts can somehow make us more godly and improve our standing before Him.

WINDOWS TO THE ANCIENT WORLD

Written Babylonian accounts of the building of the city of Babylon refer to its construction in heaven by the gods as a celestial city, as an expression of pride. These accounts say it was made by the same process of brick-making described in [Genesis 11:3], with every brick inscribed with the name of the Babylonian god Marduk. Also the ziggurat, the step-like tower believed to have been first erected in Babylon, was said to have its top in the heavens. This artificial mountain became the center of worship in the city, a miniature temple being at the top of the tower. The Babylonians took great pride in their building; they boasted of their city as not only impregnable, but also as the heavenly city, *babili* ("the gate of God").[3]

—*The Bible Knowledge Commentary*

How does the popular idea that "God helps those who help themselves" represent a gospel of works rather than a gospel of grace?

_____

_____

_____

In what areas do you tend to trust your own strength more than rely on God? What subtle untruths undermine your dependence on Him?

_____

_____

_____

_____

If you choose to knock down your self-made towers and let God build your life upon truth, you will find that the foundation of the world's philosophy differs vastly from your own. In his poem "The Present Crisis," James Russell Lowell, a contemporary of William Ernest Henley's, proposed that a life grounded in truth and resting upon God supersedes the kind of independent life heralded in "Invictus."

THE PRESENT CRISIS

Truth forever on the scaffold,
Wrong forever on the throne —
Yet that scaffold sways the future, and,
behind the dim unknown,
Standeth God within the shadow,
Keeping watch above his own.[4]

Lowell knew the truth that Henley missed. While people like Henley who don't know the truth concentrate on promoting themselves, people like Lowell allow God's grace to hold them up. They know that the only One who deserves the credit for their success is God. They understand that there is no such thing as a self-made man because it is God who made the men and allowed for their survival and success. Therefore, He deserves the credit. Any man who gives himself the credit is a thief because he robs the glory from God and claims that he did something he did not do.

BELIEVING: THE FAITH TEST

Let's take a minute to turn to Romans 4 to meet Abraham—a man who, unlike the people of Shinar, came to understand who deserved the credit for his righteousness.

Abraham came from a family who trusted man-made idols. He was a sinner in that he followed his own desires rather than God's ways. He desperately needed to be rescued from his emptiness and resuscitated from his spiritual death.

Read Romans 4:1–5. Was Abraham made right before God based on his works? Who declared Abraham righteous? On what basis?

_____

_____

_____

_____

If you are a believer in Jesus Christ, you enjoy freedom from condemnation for sin (Romans 8:1). Who deserves the credit for your right standing before God? Why?

_____

_____

_____

If you have always trusted in yourself to earn your right standing before God, do you think you will you go to heaven? Why or why not?

_____

_____

_____

_____

According to Romans 5:1, the only way to have right standing before God and be with Him in heaven is to believe in Christ—to have faith that His death will cover our wrongs. Then, we will have peace with God, not because of our works, but because of His sacrifice on the cross. It is His work on the cross that pays our way to heaven, and all who accept His

Justification is the sovereign act of God whereby He declares righteous the believing sinner—while he is still in a sinning state. Even though Abraham (after believing and being justified) would continue to sin from time to time, God heard Abraham when he said, "I believe . . . I believe in You."

—The Grace Awakening

payment for their sins receive the free gift of eternal life. All those who do not accept His payment for their sins will have to pay for their own sins when they die.

EXPLAINING: GRACE FOR THE SINFUL

No amount of education, reading, or churchgoing will take away our problem of sin. We are contaminated with it.

According to Romans 5:12, what happened to all of mankind when sin entered the world through Adam?

_____

_____

_____

_____

Because Adam sinned, we all have sinned. Therefore, we all need forgiveness; we all need a Savior. Romans 5:18–19 shows us this Savior.

Read Romans 5:18–19. What does Christ's act of obedience in His life and through His death on the cross offer to all?

_____

_____

_____

_____

Because Jesus followed God in obedience, became a man, lived a sinless life, and died an undeserved death on the cross, those who believe in Him will have right standing before God. That's grace. Once we accept the grace He extends to us from above, we'll be free to reach out to other people and offer them grace. In light of all the undeserved grace He has poured on us, we can't help but let it overflow to others.

Romans 5:20 continues: "The Law came in so that the transgression would increase; but where sin increased, grace abounded all the more."

The Law was never intended to be a means of earning our way to heaven. Rather, it shows us that we can't earn our way because we can't meet the Law's standard. God's

Law shines a light on our transgressions, illuminates our guilt, and intensifies our awareness of our wrongs. The Law was never meant to help us overcome our sinfulness, but to remind us we need to be rescued. Jesus came to our rescue, and His grace gives us our freedom!

The terrors of Law and of God
With me can have nothing to do;
My Savior's obedience and blood
Hide all my transgressions from view"[5]

—Augustus Toplady

Romans 5:21 concludes, "So that, as sin reigned in death, even so grace would reign through righteousness to eternal life through Jesus Christ our Lord."

Just as sin reigned supreme, carrying the reality of death, grace reigns in highest authority, offering the free gift of righteousness.

 Where sin overflowed, grace flooded in.

 Where sin measurably increased, grace immeasurably increased.

 Where sin was finite, grace was infinite.

 Where sin was colossal, grace was super-colossal.

Exploring: My Past and My Future

Do you ever wonder what part we play in our salvation? Let's turn to Ephesians 2:1–9 and find out.

Read Ephesians 2:1–9. Since you were dead before you accepted Christ, did you play any part in bringing yourself to life in Christ?

_____

_____

_____

How much credit does verse 8 give us for being alive together with Christ?

_____

_____

_____

(Note that Ephesians 2 addresses a group of people who have already accepted God's grace. If you haven't accepted God's grace, you're still dead in your sins. That is, you have never by faith received Jesus Christ and His gift of life.)

If we give ourselves credit for our salvation or our growth in Christ, we're still subscribing to the heresy of humanism. Deep down, a part of us, like Ernest Henley, still thinks we're the captains of our own souls. When we truly understand that the only part we played in our salvation was the part of a sinner in need of a rescuer, we will humble ourselves and pay tribute to the true Captain of our souls:

MY CAPTAIN

Out of the light that dazzles me,
Bright as the sun from pole to pole,
I thank the God I know to be
For Christ the conqueror of my soul.

Since His the sway of circumstance,
I would not wince nor cry aloud.
Under the rule which men call chance
My head with joy is humbly bowed.

Beyond this place of sin and tears
That Life with Him! And His the aid,
Despite the menace of the years,
Keeps, and shall keep me, unafraid.

I have no fear, though strait the gate,
He cleared from punishment the scroll.
Christ is the Master of my fate,
Christ is the captain of my soul.[6]

— DOROTHEA DAY

Spreading Your Wings

Have you ever trusted Christ to be the Master of your fate? The Captain of your soul? If not, you can do it now. Use the space below to tell Him that you want to turn from yourself and turn to Him as Captain as you accept His gift of grace.

_____

_____

_____

_____

_____

_____

If you have already trusted Christ to be the Captain of your soul, are you letting Him steer your soul completely? If not, in what areas do you need to put the wheel back in His hands?

_____

_____

_____

_____

_____

_____

_____

People who credit *themselves* for what they have accomplished for God don't understand grace. They're humanists at heart. Their man-centered theology pours on the pressure. They'll tell you that you have to try harder to succeed in your Christian life. These grace killers mistakenly think that what they do affects what God does for them. Don't let them load you down with to-dos. God gives us salvation freely when we believe. And, once we believe, it's His work as Captain of our souls that makes us more like Christ.

The duties God requires of us are not in proportion
to the strength we possess in ourselves.
Rather, they are proportional to the resources
available to us in Christ.
We do not have the ability in ourselves
to accomplish the least of God's tasks.[7]

—JOHN OWEN

3

ISN'T GRACE RISKY?

 Soaring on His Word

What shall we say then? Are we to continue in sin so that grace
may increase? May it never be! How shall we who died to sin
still live in it?

—ROMANS 6:1–2

H AVE YOU EVER HEARD THE EXPRESSION "Give them an inch, and they'll take a mile"? Many Christians say the same thing about grace: "Offer people free grace, and they'll run wild with it." They'll run out of the church and back to gorging themselves on their sinful desires. These grace killers undermine the message of grace by putting a price on the gift that God gives for free. They attach a price tag by emphasizing works over grace, by handing out lists of dos and don'ts, by leaving no room for any gray areas, or by judging those who may not agree or cooperate with their plan.

If you choose to follow another way of thinking, they'll say you're not a committed Christ-follower. They'd rather get you to pay for God's grace (an impossibility, actually) than risk the possibility that you'll use grace as a get-to-sin-for-free card. In their zeal to keep everyone from sin, they actually embrace evil by corrupting the gospel.

Responding to this false gospel of conditional grace, one famous preacher at London's Westminster Chapel, Dr. Martyn Lloyd-Jones, challenged his fellow ministers not to underestimate how radical God's grace is. The wise minister turned to the apostle Paul's question at the beginning of Romans 6 ("Are we to continue in sin that grace may increase?") and said that the fact that some use grace as an excuse to indulge their selfish desires shows that the message of grace is being rightly heralded.

> *If it is true that where sin abounded grace has much more abounded, well then, "shall we continue in sin, that grace may abound yet further"?*
>
> The true preaching of the gospel of salvation by grace alone always leads to the possibility of this charge being brought against it. There is no better test as to whether a man is really preaching the New Testament gospel of salvation than this, that some people might misunderstand it and misinterpret it to mean that . . . because you are saved by grace alone it does not matter at all what you do; you can go on sinning as much as you like because it will redound all the more to the glory of grace. That is a very good test of gospel preaching. If my preaching and presentation of the gospel of salvation does not expose it to that misunderstanding, then it is not the gospel.[1]
>
> — Dr. Martyn Lloyd-Jones

The English evangelical was right. Grace is risky. In fact, it's dangerous for the very reason his critics said it was—because some people will misunderstand it and take it as a license to continue sinning. That's why the legalists fear it. While they'll never be accused of preaching a grace that people might abuse, they'll also never experience the true liberty that grace can bring.

THE REALITY OF RISK

So, how does the believer who wants to experience grace as God intended deal with the risky side of grace? Does this free gift loose us to run wild? Or will it require us to fence ourselves in with legalistic rules to keep sin locked out of our lives?

Statement of Clarification

Let's look back at a verse of Scripture we studied in chapter 2. Romans 5:1 says, "Therefore having been justified by faith, we have peace with God through our Lord Jesus Christ."

God sovereignly bestows the gift of eternal life on the sinner who believes and declares the sinner righteous. The person hasn't stopped sinning. He or she has only recognized a need to be rescued from sin and has believed that God is the One who can rescue him or her through Jesus's death and resurrection. The sinner who believes brings no pledges of right living, no vows to give up all worldly possessions to follow Christ, no promissory note to be paid out over time. God finds him or her with a sin-stained heart and empty hands and offers to take away the sin and change the heart. The sinner has not sworn never to sin again. He or she has changed his or her mind toward Christ *(repentance)* and simply received the gift of eternal life through faith in Jesus. Because of Christ, God declares the

GETTING TO THE ROOT

The Greek noun *metanoia* translated "repentance" in the New Testament literally means a "change of mind." Wendell Johnston writes, "The context determines the purpose for the change," and notes that "when the term *repentance* was used in relation to salvation it was almost an interchangeable synonym for faith, rather than an action distinct from faith."[2] Therefore, repentance is not to be understood as changing your lifestyle, doing good deeds, or even committing to a holy life. It is a change of mind about Christ and His work, choosing to trust in Him instead of self.

believer righteous *(justification)*, and then He begins the day-by-day, bit-by-bit process of growing that person toward maturity *(sanctification)*.

Spreading Your Wings

Though life as a Christian is not easy, God's grace is
Really Just Simple.

The moment we
Repent, He
Justifies us. Then He spends the rest of our lives
Sanctifying us.

Now, it's your turn to see if you understand how Really Just Simple His grace is.

1. *Multiple Choice.* In order to repent, sinners have to
   a. get their lives right and then ask God to forgive them for the things they've done wrong.
   b. take the gift of grace that God offers through faith in Jesus Christ and never run back to the sins they used to do.
   c. change their minds about Jesus Christ and take the gift of grace that God offers through faith in Him.

2. *True or False.* God declares believing sinners righteous when they believe, but once they believe, believing sinners can lose their right standing before God when they sin.

3. Read Hebrews 10:10–18. God sanctifies us through what offering?

4. Whose sacrifice covers all of the believing sinner's past, present, and future sins?

Answers: 1. c   2. False   3. Jesus's blood   4. Jesus's

The privilege to believe grace in its fullness and to live grace in its fullness guarantees that some will take advantage of it. People who take grace for granted believe that because grace is free, it's cheap. They fail to understand that, though it costs the believer nothing, it cost God His Son and it cost Jesus His life. They abuse grace and run back to their sin. But the fear that grace abusers will consider free grace to be a license for sin doesn't give anyone the right to stifle the message of grace. In spite of the very real risks, the message of free grace must be shared.

ALTERNATIVES TO GRACE

Sometimes our fear tempts us to join the grace killers. If we choose to censor the message of the gospel and put a price tag on grace, we may adopt four popular grace-killing tendencies:

 We may emphasize works over grace.

 We may make a list of moral dos and don'ts.

 We may leave no room for any gray areas in our lives or in others'.

 We may cultivate a judgmental attitude toward those who may not agree or cooperate with our plans.

Have others' lists of moral dos and don'ts stunted your spiritual growth by pressuring you to measure your spiritual condition by how well you jump through their hoops? How does the weight of their expectations make you feel?

_____

_____

_____

_____

_____

Are you stunting someone else's spiritual growth with your list or critical spirit? How will you drop your critical attitude and point that person toward true holiness?

_____

_____

_____

_____

> Jay Kesler, president of Taylor University, told me about his own brush with legalism. Shortly after deciding to follow Christ as a teenager, he felt overwhelmed by all the new rules imposed on him. Confused, Jay walked around his backyard in Indiana and noticed his faithful collie Laddy, merrily gnawing on a bone while stretched out in the glistening wet grass. It struck Jay that Laddy was possibly the best Christian he knew. Laddy did not smoke, drink, go to movies, dance, or carry protest signs. He was harmless, docile, and inactive. At once Jay saw how far he had strayed from the life of freedom and passion to which Jesus had called him.[3]
>
> — PHILIP YANCEY

Once we accept God's gift of grace, we're free! Free from evil's reign. Free from guilt and shame. Free from the damnable desires we couldn't say no to when sin mastered us. Free to obey. Free to love. Free to live beyond the limitations of human effort!

FLYING AGAINST THE WINDS OF OUR CULTURE

We love the law when we're the offended and loathe it when we're the offenders. If a driver speeds through the stop sign at Third and Main and crashes into the passenger door of our sleek sports car, we call the police. But if we're the one zipping through a red light and racing to work because we hit the snooze button one too many times, we hope the cops are nowhere near. When we're wrong, we cry for mercy. When we're wronged, we demand justice.

That's why so many people don't understand God's grace. It's not in our nature to take another person's guilt and suffer in his or her place. Divine grace makes no earthly sense to us! The gospel message is so astounding that some people never believe it, and those who do believe still marvel that the gift we don't deserve is completely free.

It's unbelievable! It's marvelous! And it's true! The guilty who believe in the Innocent Son are pardoned because, in taking our punishment upon Himself, He satisfied justice and showered us with abundant life—extending to us forgiveness and inviting us to call Him Brother (see Hebrews 2:11).

THE INESCAPABLE TENSION

Grace emancipates us from sin's yoke and breaks the chains of our selfish attitudes, urges, and actions. But our newfound freedom creates a certain tension. It gives us the choice to turn from sin or to return to sin. Once we are living by grace, we can take our liberty to extremes and indulge in a life of license.

The apostle Paul addressed this tension in Romans 6:1–15. He opened his argument in verse 1 with the question most people ask when they learn that grace is free: "What shall we say then? Are we to continue in sin so that grace may increase?"

While it may seem at first glance that grace gives us free reign to gorge ourselves on sin, Paul's words challenge us to look deeper to see that grace gives us the freedom to say no to the sin that used to master us. Let's consider Paul's response to that all-important question in the verses that follow. We'll take a closer look at each section in the questions below.

Romans 6:2–7

Why are people who have accepted God's grace dead to sin? What happened that has freed us from being slaves to sin?

_____

_____

_____

_____

If you're a believer in Jesus Christ, how can knowing that you have been freed from the power of sin affect your daily life?

_____

_____

_____

_____

Romans 6:8–11

When we were set free from sin through belief in Christ, our old selves (our former natures) died, never to return. We now live with the presence of the Holy Spirit in our hearts, guiding and enabling us to live more like Christ. How did Christ live?

_____

_____

_____

_____

As a believer, how does the fact that you are free and fully able to say no to sin and yes to God make you want to live?

_____

_____

_____

_____

Romans 6:12–15

If you are a believer in Jesus, you have the ability to say no to sin, but you still have the choice of whether you'll let sin reign in your life. Even with this freedom to choose to live for God, why is it so tempting to let sin continue to reign?

_____

_____

_____

_____

When you choose to let sin reign in your life, what is the effect on you?

_____

_____

_____

_____

When you choose to follow God and say no to sin, what is the effect of that decision on your life?

_____

_____

_____

_____

There is a principle that is even higher than the principle of liberty—it's love. It's servanthood. Paul wrote in Galatians 5:13–16:

> For you were called to freedom, brethren; only do not turn your freedom into an opportunity for the flesh, but through love serve one another. For the whole Law is fulfilled in one word, in the statement, "You shall love your neighbor as yourself." But if you bite and devour one another, take care that you are not consumed by one another. But I say, walk by the Spirit, and you will not carry out the desire of the flesh.

We must temper our liberty with self-control and restraint to ensure that we don't become irresponsible in the way we live in grace.

The Benefits of Liberty

 No longer helplessly bound by impulses and desires

 Free to make your own choices

 Able to think independently without the tyranny of comparison or the need to control

 Able to grow more rapidly toward greater maturity and flexibility, becoming the person you were meant to be

The Dangers of Liberty

- A lack of love for others . . . little care about anybody else

- A rationalization of out-and-out sin

- An unwillingness to be accountable

- A resistance to anyone getting close enough to give them wise advice

- A disregard for one who is a new convert and therefore weak in faith—but beware of the grace killer who acts like a weaker brother, but is really a legalist

The Proper Use of Liberty

Serve One Another in Love

Under the liberty of grace, our behavior is restrained not by rules, but by relationship. We make decisions from a heart of love for others and for God. How does responsible liberty look in practice? The following story illustrates.

> I remember when I first earned my license to drive. I was about sixteen. . . .
>
> I'll never forget the day I came in, flashed my newly acquired permit, and said, "Dad, look!" . . . Holding the keys to his car, he tossed them in my direction and smiled. "Tell you what, Son . . . you can have the car for two hours, all on your own." . . .
>
> I thanked him, danced out to the garage, opened the car door, and shoved the key into the ignition. . . . While cruising along "all on my own," I began to think wild stuff—like, *This car can probably do 100 miles an hour. I could go to Galveston and back twice in two hours if I averaged 100 miles an hour. I can fly down the Gulf Freeway and even run a few lights. After all, nobody's here to say, "Don't!"* We're talking dangerous, crazy thoughts! But you know what? I didn't do any of them. I don't believe I drove above the speed limit. In fact, I distinctly remember turning into the driveway early . . . didn't even stay away the full two hours. Amazing, huh? I had my dad's car all to myself with a full gas tank in a context of total privacy and freedom, but I didn't go crazy. Why? My relationships with my dad and my granddad were so strong that I couldn't, even though I had a license and nobody was in the car to restrain me. Over a period of time there had developed a sense of trust, a deep love relationship that held me in restraint.
>
> — *The Grace Awakening*

Suggestions for Living Freely and Responsibly

The freedom we have in Christ is not the freedom to do anything we want, but to be everything God created us to be. To be everything God created us to be, we must pursue a life of grace, not chasing our lusts, but rather honoring Him with our righteousness. Here are some suggestions for doing just that.

 Enjoy the freedom grace provides. Your liberty is a gift from God. There's no reason to feel guilty about what God has given us to enjoy (1 Timothy 4:4–5). Give yourself permission to be free.

Treat grace as an undeserved privilege rather than an exclusive right. Be grateful about what God has done for you, not arrogant or demanding about it.

 Remember that while grace came to you freely, it cost the Savior His life. We handle with care what comes at a great cost. Handle your liberty that way. It came to you at the cost of Jesus's life.

God sent His Son not only to forgive us but also to set us free. He knew what he was doing. He knew that we could learn to live responsibly in the context of liberty. He knew that, in the end, rules would not change us—relationship would. As we come to know "the God of all grace" (1 Peter 5:10), we love Him all the more. We love our freedom. And, in our freedom, we love others. Just as our Father does.

No one can be good and do good unless
God's grace first makes him good, and no one becomes good by works,
but good works are done only by him who is good.
Just so the fruits do not make the tree, but the tree bears the fruit. . . .
Therefore all works, no matter how good they are and
how pretty they look, are in vain if they do not flow from grace. [4]

—MARTIN LUTHER

4

UNDESERVING, YET
UNCONDITIONALLY LOVED

 Soaring on His Word

> *But by the grace of God, I am what I am, and His grace toward*
> *me did not prove vain; but I labored even more than all of*
> *them, yet not I, but the grace of God with me.*
>
> — 1 CORINTHIANS 15:10

*H*ONK! HONK! The blaring horn of an eighteen-wheeler jolted Sam awake. The sound of the wheels rolling across the bridge overhead reverberated in his ears. A mangy alley dog scavenged through the trash looking for something to eat. The mutt stuck his nose in a McDonald's carton but found no fries. Sam had beaten him to the stale potato sticks an hour earlier. Sam's rumbling stomach reminded him how long it had been since he'd had a hot meal. He could still taste the homemade pot roast and sugar cookies he loved as a child. If the boy who had eaten his fill of cookies, chased his dog over every hill of his family's thirty-acre estate, and pretended to run his grand-father's *Fortune* 500 company from his treehouse could see himself grown up, he wouldn't recognize this homeless vagrant.

Sam passed the rest of the night thinking about how much better his life would have been had his grandfather not gotten so power hungry and lost his multimillion-dollar company and then crashed his Mercedes.

A moment of recklessness had taken away Sam's father and grandfather—all the family he'd ever known. Six weeks after his grandfather's and father's funerals, the bank had foreclosed on the house Sam called home. After the movers had loaded the last of the boxes, the nanny had scooped young Sam up and had started down the stairs of the front porch. Catching her heel on the next-to-last step, she had fallen hard against the sidewalk.

Now, thirty years later, Sam can't remember hitting the concrete, but he's reminded of the crushing blow every time he struggles to get around. Everyone says it's a miracle that he's alive. Some miracle! The man born into privilege now spends every day trapped in a wheelchair, panhandling on the corner. When traffic is slow, he reads day-old *Wall Street Journals* that he finds in the trash. This morning, there's another headline heralding the success of Davis Dawnsby, the renowned business-man who replaced his grandfather as CEO.

As the subway delivered its first load of pinstriped professionals to their downtown destination, commuters pour onto the sidewalk. Most of them avoid making eye con-tact with Sam, but one briefcase-carrying businessman looks right at him. Sam seizes the opportunity, "Excuse me, Mister. Can you spare some change?"

Ignoring the question, the impeccably dressed man in a black suit and red silk tie asks, "Are you Sam Whittle? The grandson of Walter Whittle?"

"Who wants to know?"

"Davis Dawnsby."

Great! thinks Sam. *The man who has it all has come to gloat.* "Yeah. That's me. The last living heir of the infamous W. Whittle. I'm the golden boy with a corner office on the curb. What do you want?"

"I've been searching for you since I learned that you were still living. I want to give you stock in my company, a luxury corporate apartment, and a seat on my executive board."

Sam stares at the distinguished man in disbelief. "You've got to be kidding! My grandfather tried to force you out of the company when you were a promising young executive. Why would you want to give me a thing?"

"It's true. Your grandfather did plot my demise, but your father was my best friend. He opposed your grandfather and protected me. A long time ago, I promised your father that I would always care for his household. Since you're his only heir, I want to offer you a place with me."

This may sound like an unbelievable Cinderella story, but it's no fairy tale. Instead, it's a modern-day retelling of the true Old Testament account about Mephibosheth—a man who experienced overwhelming grace.

Before we meet this man whose world turned upside down on the day his family fell from greatness, let's hear a testimony of grace from a New Testament man named Paul—a man who found his purpose in following Christ. This former persecutor of Christians became a devoted Christ-follower when he finally understood God's grace. Paul also noted that our relationships with others should be marked by God's grace. Listen to the apostle's words:

> For I am the least of the apostles, and not fit to be called an apostle, because I persecuted the church of God. But by the grace of God I am what I am, and His grace toward me did not prove vain; but I labored even more than all of them, yet not I, but the grace of God with me. Whether then it was I or they, so we preach and so you believed. (1 Corinthians 15:9–11)

REAFFIRMING THE TRUTH OF GRACE

The man called "the great apostle" knew himself well. Because he never forgot who he had been before Jesus found him, he lived his life according to a three-part credo of humility.

First: God does what He does by grace. As a man who prided himself on his intelligence, his accomplishments, and the ruthless murders of innocent first-century Christians, Paul deserved severe judgment. Instead, God forgave him and used him to herald the gospel to the entire known world.

Second: I am what I am by the grace of God. Unlike many Christians today, Paul recognized that God deserved the credit for the good things that the apostle did. A man who knows himself as well as Paul did will credit grace for his accomplishments. While most of our cultural heroes credit themselves for their success, Paul's words challenge us to acknowledge the One who literally made us who we are.

Third: I let you be who you are by the grace of God. Just as God is the One who shapes us, we need to allow Him to be the One to mold those around us. Since God gives us undeserved grace, we need to extend it to others rather than trying to turn them into whom we think they should be.

Jesus spoke of an abundant life that we enter into when we accept His grace. Wouldn't it be wonderful if people cooperated with that game plan? If they would turn off their negativity and hold their tongues rather than confronting us when they find just one flaw, discover a single failure, or uncover a slight shortcoming in us? Often, grace killers impose their rules on us because they think their way is the only road to growth.

In what ways have you experienced God's grace in your life and in your relationships?

_____

_____

_____

_____

_____

_____

Do you find it easy or difficult to let people be who they are? Why do you think this is the case?

_____

_____

_____

_____

_____

Do you at times find yourself being harder on family members or people at work than, in retrospect, you wanted to be? In which of your relationships is this an issue?

_____

_____

_____

_____

_____

FLYING AGAINST THE WINDS OF OUR CULTURE

Often, the important people in our lives criticize us in an effort to change us for the better. Unfortunately, harsh words and unreasonable demands often produce the opposite effect. In an article "People Grow Better in Grace," Jackie Hudson writes of one such occurrence in her own life.

> Early in my career I had a boss who held to numerous spoken and unspoken rules. One was that I needed to have my lights out by 11 p.m. so I wouldn't be tired on the job the next day. His house wasn't far from mine, and if he noticed my lights on after 11, I heard about it the next morning.
>
> I remember my first compliment from him—a full year after I'd been on the job. I'd been given a project, and I worked night and day to make it perfect and, thus, win his approval.
>
> The day of the event he wanted all the other employees to arrive an hour early to help with preparations. Even after I explained that it wouldn't be necessary, he insisted. After all the employees stood around for an hour with nothing to do, the program began. I couldn't have been more pleased with the event. The project was flawless.
>
> Afterward my boss walked up to me, looked down at the floor, and out of his mouth came those long-awaited words: "Well done, Miss Hudson." My year in that environment brought on a remarkable response: rebellion.
>
> I was hardly growing in grace. Grace is fertile soil . . . .
>
> Grace focuses on who God is and what He has done, and takes the focus off ourselves. And yet it's so easy to think we need to do something to earn God's favor, as though grace is too good to be true. [1]

Grace provides the environment that makes growth possible—in human relationships and in our relationships with God. In fact, the degree to which we experience God's grace usually governs the degree to which we extend grace to others and to ourselves.

When have you found yourself trying to perform for God the way that Jackie Hudson performed for her boss? How did this make you feel?

_____

_____

_____

_____

How is God different from Jackie's boss? How do you know?

_____

_____

_____

_____

Growth-stunting grace killers will always try to give you lists on how you should live your life. They will use guilt to manipulate you until you feel that you're about to go mad. Don't let them have the keys to your mind! Remember that God never uses guilt to shame or manipulate us. Others might, but He doesn't. We are who we are by the grace of God. You who really understand this truth will let God guide you to His destination for your life.

If Paul had no lists, who are we to make them? Unlike our Lord, we much prefer to give people what they deserve rather than the grace that they *don't* deserve. "You get what you pay for," we say. "Nothing's for free!" Many of us are quicker to criticize than we are to praise. All of us tend to put conditions on grace. Though we're ready to drink in grace for ourselves, we're quick to deprive others of its refreshment. Be certain to represent God's grace accurately—even if it seems risky!

MEET MEPHIBOSHETH

Now that we've explored the New Testament teaching on grace, let's step into the time tunnel, travel back in time three thousand years to days of Eastern dynasties, and drop in on Mephibosheth, the grandson of a king.

It so happened that Saul's son, Jonathan, had a son who was maimed in both feet. When he was five years old, the report on Saul and Jonathan came from Jezreel. His nurse picked him up and ran, but in her hurry to get away she fell, and the boy was maimed. His name was Mephibosheth. (2 Samuel 4:4 MSG)

Mephibosheth was the son of Jonathan and the grandson of Saul, the king of Israel. When King Saul and his sons died in battle against the Philistines, his family's hold on the throne ended (1 Samuel 31:1–6). In those days, when a dynasty fell, its family members were killed to ensure the security of the next dynasty. Therefore, when Saul died in battle, his household assumed their lives were in danger and fled.

The nurse's hurry came at a high price for five-year-old Mephibosheth. Made permanently lame by his fall, the grandson of a once-honored king would live in virtual obscurity for the next fifteen to twenty years.

A QUESTION ASKED

We hear about Mephibosheth again in chapter 9 of 2 Samuel. Now an adult, the crippled man watched as his grandfather's successor, David, assumed the throne and won the hearts of the nation. The Jewish people sang David's praises throughout the land. At this time, God's anointed king had garnered an unblemished reputation, expanded his territory from six thousand to sixty thousand square miles, built the strongest military in Israel's history, won every battle he'd waged, and watched the economy bloom under his rule. God had graciously given him prosperity and blessing.

As David reflected upon the blessings God had given him, he asked, "Is there anyone left of Saul's family? If so, I'd like to show him some kindness in honor of Jonathan" (2 Samuel 9:1 MSG).

It's a question asked by a grateful man. If you've ever thought back fondly on a significant relationship with a person who played an important role in your life, with a desire to express your appreciation to that individual, then you know what David was feeling. He remembered that when Jonathan was still alive, he and Jonathan had promised to protect each other even though Jonathan's father, Saul, was plotting to kill David. Jonathan swore to David,

As GOD, the God of Israel, is my witness, by this time tomorrow I'll get it out of my father how he feels about you. Then I'll let you know what I learn. May GOD do his worst to me if I let you down! If my father still intends to kill you, I'll tell you and get you out of here in one piece. And GOD be with you as he's been with my father! If I make it through this alive, continue to be my covenant friend. And if I die, keep the covenant friendship with my family—forever. And when GOD finally rids the earth of David's enemies, stay loyal to Jonathan! (1 Samuel 20:12–15 MSG)

As David reflected on his good fortune years later, the memory of the promise flashed back to him. Since Jonathan was dead, David wondered if there was any living member of Saul's household to whom he might show *chesed*—the Hebrew word often rendered "mercy," "lovingkindness," or "grace" in the Old Testament. David wasn't looking for someone who merited blessing. He wasn't seeking someone deserving. He wanted *anyone*.

David's "yes"-faced question was met with a "no"-faced response from the servant Ziba:

The king asked, "Is there anyone left from the family of Saul to who I can show some godly kindness?"

Ziba told the king, "Yes, there is Jonathan's son, lame in both feet."

"Where is he?"

"He's living at the home of Makir son of Ammiel in Lo Debar."

(2 Samuel 9:3–4 MSG)

Can't you just hear the negativity in Ziba's voice? "Yes, Jonathan left one descendant, but he's crippled, and he lives in Lo-debar. We don't want to go there." *Lo-debar* literally means "a barren place" in Hebrew. But David never flinched. For him, the recipient didn't need to be strong. He didn't need to live in the right neighborhood. He just needed to be willing to receive the king's lovingkindness.

A Straggler Sought

King David didn't lose a minute. He sent and got him from the home of Makir son of Ammiel in Lo Debar.

When Mephibosheth son of Jonathan (who was the son of Saul), came before David, he bowed deeply, abasing himself, honoring David.

David spoke his name: "Mephibosheth."

"Yes, sir?"

"Don't be frightened," said David. "I'd like to do something special for you in memory of your father Jonathan. To begin with, I'm returning to you all the properties of your grandfather Saul. Furthermore, from now on you'll take all your meals at my table."

Shuffling and stammering, not looking him in the eye, Mephibosheth said, "Who am I that you pay attention to a stray dog like me?" (2 Samuel 9:5–8 MSG)

The crippled man, who had spent his life in anonymity, surely felt terrified and unworthy when he came before the king. Since the day his nurse had fled with him, Mephibosheth had spent his life hiding, certain that he'd be killed if he were discovered. But, on the contrary, the day David sent for him was the best day of his life. The king's grace released Mephibosheth from the fear that had hung over him every day since his grandfather's demise and opened to him a new life filled with lovingkindness.

Just as David allayed Mephibosheth's fear, Jesus, the One who was full of grace and truth, repeatedly commanded His followers not to fear. Amazing, isn't it? The perfect Son of God knew that the most common reaction when someone stood before Him would be fear. And, rather than bringing judgment to the guilty, He extended grace to those who would accept it.

Spreading Your Wings

Think of a time when you deserved judgment, but someone extended grace to you instead. Below, jot down what happened. How do you feel toward the person who extended grace to you?

_____

_____

_____

_____

If human lovingkindness can overwhelm us, God's divine grace should amaze and astound us. Have you ever been afraid when you've measured yourself against God's perfection? What did you fear?

_____

_____

_____

_____

How does the grace that God offered us through Jesus's death calm your fears?

_____

_____

_____

_____

A PRIVILEGE PROVIDED

Why did David want to show Mephibosheth lovingkindness? It wasn't because of his relationship with the young man. In fact, he had no knowledge of Mephibosheth's existence before Ziba told him of the man. David wanted to show grace to Mephibosheth for Jonathan's sake. The crippled son did nothing to merit David's notice. But David stooped in grace, offered him a place at the royal table, and restored to him all the riches he had lost.

David and Mephibosheth's celebration dinner reminds us of our "banqueting table" in heaven. Won't that celestial table be a sight? As we look around the table, we'll see so many faces who said "Yes." Abraham, Moses, Elijah, Deborah, Peter, Mary, Martha, Paul, "Mrs. Gray-Haired Prayer Warrior," "Mr. Missionary," "Mr. Businessman," "Mrs. Mother of Three," "Miss Kindergarten Teacher"—the list will go on. But we will all come to the table by the same invitation—grace. It's not what we did or didn't do, but what He gave. We'll all sit at His table in awesome wonder that the King sent his beloved Son to rescue us from our "Lo-debar." Together, the children of God who once felt so unworthy will spend eternity praising the One who made them worthy.

When we've been there ten thousand years,
Bright shining as the sun,
We've no less days to sing God's praise
Than when we'd first begun. [2]

—JOHN NEWTON

5

SQUARING OFF AGAINST LEGALISM

 Soaring on His Word

It was for freedom that Christ has set us free; therefore keep standing firm and do not be subject again to a yoke of slavery.

— GALATIANS 5:1

*A*UDREY ATTENDED A CHURCH that taught that women should wear only long dresses—no slacks, no jeans, and certainly no shorts! However, Audrey secretly wore casual pants when doing housework. One day, during a particularly bold moment, Audrey decided to rush to the supermarket without changing into a dress. While she scurried through the store like a mouse in a lighted room, Audrey sighted Susan, another member of the church, wearing a "proper" dress. Suddenly, Audrey felt less like a mouse and more like a deer caught in headlights. Audrey avoided Susan as long as she could, but eventually their eyes met. As the "properly attired" Susan approached, Audrey eased behind a display case that covered her from the waist down. She stood there, unmoving, until the agonizing two-minute conversation ended and she could flee the supermarket. Once home, Audrey found freedom again behind closed doors.

"Are you so foolish?"

Three young Christian men sat down in a restaurant and prayed before their meal. By the time they said "amen," two older men dressed in shabby clothes loomed over their table with broad smiles, complimenting the young men on their display of bold-

49

ness in public prayer. The two men introduced themselves politely and then asked the young men where they attended church. Upon hearing the response, they frowned and proceeded to enumerate the problems with that church—namely, the neglect of holiness. Then they showed the young men the evidence of their own holiness: the holes in their shoes and pants, indicating how they had deprived themselves of worldly goods. Even the Bible one of them pulled out to rebuke the young men with was old and torn; it opened effortlessly to its owner's "pet passages." All the while, the young men wondered whether holiness really had anything to do with the number of holes in a person's clothes.

> "Are you so foolish? Having begun by the Spirit, are you now being perfected by the flesh?" (Galatians 3:3)

DEFINITIONS OF TWO SIGNIFICANT TERMS

Arguably, this Galatians passage contains the harshest rebuke found in any of Paul's writings. He called his errant readers "foolish" (Galatians 3:1) and cursed the false teachers who were leading them astray (1:8–9). Certainly, the issue at hand was a serious one for Paul—the very heart of the gospel of grace through faith was at stake!

What was this dreaded doctrine? Legalism.

The two examples at the beginning of this chapter may sound far-fetched, but they're based on real-life stories of encounters with extreme legalism. Fear, suspicion, doubt, anxiety, hypocrisy, pride, and arrogance—these qualities characterize our "close encounters" with the alien but all-too-common force of legalism.

What's the cure to the disease of legalism? Liberty.

Before we get too far, let's take a moment to define the terms *liberty* and *legalism*. Liberty is freedom *from* doing something and freedom *to* do something. When Audrey reached the security of her home, she was free *from* the oppressive rule of always having to wear dresses. Instead, she was free *to* wear what she wanted. Believers enjoy freedom from the bondage of sin's power and from God's wrath. This freedom includes liberation from the curse of the law and its relentless demands, as well as emancipation from the fear of condemnation and an accusing conscience.

According to the following verses, from what have Christians been freed?

Acts 13:39 _____

Romans 6:7 _____

Romans 8:2 _____

The freedom of believers is also the freedom *to* do something. Freedom allows us to revel in Christ's finished work on Calvary and empowers us to become all He wants us to be, regardless of how and where He may lead others. Freedom allows us to conduct all of our activities from a motivation of Spirit-empowered love.

Read 1 Corinthians 6:12 and 10:23. What things are lawful for believers?

_____

_____

_____

_____

Legalism, on the other hand, is a prideful attitude or mentality that forces a person to conform to an artificial standard for the purpose of exalting that person. Like the two raggedy, arrogant men in the restaurant who believed that their outward poverty was a sign of true spirituality, legalists assume a place of superiority and demand that all others conform to their personal standards.

From the descriptions of liberty and legalism above, which do you feel best describes your approach to the Christian life?

____ My walk with Christ is characterized by dos and don'ts that I perform out of duty, fear of being punished, or pride of accomplishment.

____ I trust in Christ living in me for the wisdom and power to handle every situation with a loving spirit.

How do you think a legalistic approach to Christianity could stunt a believer's spiritual growth? Relate this to childrearing—how can one transition a child from rule-based discipline to the freedom to make wise decisions on their own?

_____

_____

_____

_____

Like a rogue band of pirates seeking to plunder unwary sea vessels, some legalists seek to take over churches with their skull-and-crossbones theology. For the sake of maintaining peace at any price, many Christians accept the legalists' stance and run up the white flag at the mere threat of conflict, thus exchanging truth for a lie and freedom for slavery. The Galatians modeled this unwise surrender when they, who had been set free from the law by the gospel of grace, began to return to a life of spiritual bondage.

Needless to say, Paul was shocked. He asked, "You were running well; who hindered you from obeying the truth?" (Galatians 5:7). He wasn't about to stand by while people perverted the gospel and led his flock astray. Instead, he went on the offensive: "You foolish Galatians, who has bewitched you, before whose eyes Jesus Christ was publicly portrayed as crucified?" (Galatians 3:1).

What insidious means and treacherous tools did the false teachers use to bewitch the foolish Galatians? Let's take a hard look at three of these tools, because they're the same legalistic grace killers used today to squash the liberty we have in Christ.

IDENTIFYING THREE TOOLS OF LEGALISM

The weapons of heresy, harassment, and hypocrisy fill the arsenal used by legalists to assault the liberty of denominations, churches, and individuals. All of these weapons were used by the legalists in Paul's conflict with them, recorded in the first two chapters of Galatians.

Doctrinal Heresy

In the first few paragraphs of Galatians, Paul defended the gospel against the first weapon of the legalists: doctrinal heresy.

WINDOWS TO THE ANCIENT WORLD

The chief "pirates" of the gospel in Galatians were known as "Judaizers," and their specific heresy plagued the church for over a century. E. F. Harrison defines Judaizing as "the process of adopting Jewish religious and cultural practices, whether by choice or through coercion."[1] Nearly fifty years later, Ignatius, the pastor of Antioch, warned another church in Asia Minor about this same threat: "It is utterly absurd to profess Jesus Christ and to practice Judaism."[2] Some taught that a Gentile had to be circumcised and adhere to the Mosaic Law to please God. To Paul, who understood the grace of God, such a view was literally "accursed" (Galatians 1:8–9).

> I am amazed that you are so quickly deserting Him who called you by the grace of Christ, for a different gospel; which is really not another; only there are some who are disturbing you and want to distort the gospel of Christ. (Galatians 1:6–7)

The gospel teaches salvation *by grace through faith,* not by works, but as a gift from God (see Ephesians 2:8–9). Salvation is received by grace through faith in Christ *plus nothing.* Yet legalists come along and say, "Faith is fine, but it's not enough. You also need _____." Some fill in the blank with "good works," others say "baptism," still others say "membership in our particular religious group." In Paul's day, the Judaizers filled in the blank with "circumcision." Good works and baptism are important, but they don't earn us salvation or merit with God. Rather, they are the *results* of a Spirit-filled life, not the *cause* of it (see Ephesians 2:10).

What "additions" to the simple gospel of salvation by grace through faith in Christ alone have you encountered in the past?

_____

_____

_____

Why do you think people have such a hard time believing that salvation is truly free?

_____

_____

_____

_____

In Galatians 1:8–9, Paul twice said that those who teach a gospel of works are "accursed." Paul wanted to make his readers understand clearly that such a distortion of the gospel must not be tolerated for a moment. The apostle believed that some things were worth fighting for, and this was one of them. He wrote, "For am I now seeking the favor of men, or of God? Or am I striving to please men? If I were still trying to please men, I would not be a bond-servant of Christ" (Galatians 1:10).

 GETTING TO THE ROOT

The Greek term for "accursed" is *anathema,* the strongest Greek word Paul could use to condemn false teaching.[3] Paul used the same word in Romans 9:3 to mean "separated" from Christ. In 1 Corinthians 16:22, Paul also wrote, "If anyone does not love the Lord, he is to be accursed." This type of condemnation was reserved for the most serious, eternally significant offenses, by which certain people attempted to destroy the very heart of the gospel.

Ecclesiastical Harassment

The second tool of legalists is *harassment.* This grace-killing tactic is used by those who spy out and enslave unwitting believers. We see an example of this in Galatians 2:1–6. Paul told the Galatians how he, Barnabas (a Jew), and Titus (a Gentile) had conferred with the original apostles—including Peter—about the gospel in order to confirm that they were united in their message (2:1–2, 6). However, among the Jerusalem church were "false brethren" who had sneaked in to "spy out" the liberty they had in Christ (2:4). Paul wrote concerning them, "But we did not yield in subjection to them for even an hour, so that the truth of the gospel might remain with you" (2:5).

In Galatians 2:4, the Greek word translated *spy out* means "lie in wait for," implying a treacherous activity.[4] The same word is used in 2 Samuel 10:3 to describe activity associated with plotting to overthrow a city. The legalists intended to find ways to accuse Paul and his companions, thus overthrowing the Christian's freedom.

Things haven't changed much, have they? Today, legalists infiltrate churches, wrestle to snatch the helms of ministries, and try to steer Christians down the path of spiritual corruption.

For biblical examples of legalists, read the following passages and note some of their characteristics.

1 Timothy 4:2–3

_____

_____

_____

_____

3 John 9–10

_____

_____

_____

_____

Have you encountered legalists in the past? Describe their character traits.

_____

_____

_____

Personal Hypocrisy

The third weapon of the grace killer is *hypocrisy.* Hypocrites lie and deceive, waffle over important issues, and appear chameleon-like in their manners. As you read Galatians 2, you may be shocked at the example Paul used to warn his readers of this threat. He relayed to them the hypocrisy of Peter, who had come to Antioch to visit Paul and other "apostles to the Gentiles." While there, Peter enjoyed his Christian liberty, eating with Gentiles (something that was forbidden by the rigid commands of Judaism). Everything was fine until some Jewish brothers arrived and began pressuring Peter to conform to Jewish traditions. Fearing the disapproval of the legalistic Judaizers, Peter withdrew from the Gentile believers. Others followed his example—even Paul's companion, Barnabas (Galatians 2:11–13). For this hypocrisy, Paul rebuked Peter publicly, and he had every right to do so (Galatians 2:14–21).

DIGGING DEEPER

Most Christians agree that justification (initial salvation) occurs by grace through faith in Christ alone. However, on the subject of sanctification (growing in Christ), some have abandoned the true gospel for the heresy Paul so strongly refutes. Many people erroneously believe that once they become Christians by faith, they must follow a new list of rules and regulations in order to please God—not to be saved, but to grow in Christ or to stay on God's "good side." The liberating truth is that not only are we saved by grace through faith (Ephesians 2:8–9), but our spiritual growth is also a gift from God received by grace through faith (2:10). The gospel of grace for the sinner's salvation is the same gospel of grace for the saint's sanctification.[5]

Paul clearly addressed this truth in Galatians 3:2–3. He wrote, "This only I want to learn from you: Did you receive the Spirit by the works of the law, or by the hearing of faith?" The answer to this rhetorical question, of course, is "by the hearing of faith" (NKJV). This covers the Galatians' initial salvation.

Paul then wrote, "Are you so foolish? Having begun in the Spirit, are you now being made perfect by the flesh?" The phrase "being made perfect" (*epiteleō* in Greek) means to "bring to an end" or "finish."[6] The present-tense verb indicates a continuing process—the people's present experience as believers. Paul used the same verb to describe believers' spiritual growth in Philippians 1:6, where he told his readers, "He who has begun a good work in you *will complete it* until the day of Jesus Christ" (NKJV, emphasis added). God began the work by grace, and He will complete it by grace.

After trusting Christ for freedom from the guilt of sin, have you now transferred your trust back to yourself for freedom from sin's power? Paul asked the Galatians who were guilty of the same thing, "Are you so foolish?" (Galatians 3:3).

How can our hypocrisy have a damaging effect on the faith and spiritual lives of those who look to us for leadership?

_____

_____

_____

_____

_____

How do the examples of Peter's and Barnabas's brief lapses into hypocrisy and legalism warn us about our own susceptibility to fall into the same trap? In your answer, consider the circumstances that led these men to this point.

_____

_____

_____

_____

_____

Read Paul's rebuke of Peter's hypocrisy in Galatians 2:14–21. What does Paul say is the source of godly, Christlike living once a person is saved by grace?

_____

_____

_____

_____

If we want to experience a grace awakening in our lives, we must, like Paul, prepare ourselves to square off against legalism and its weapons of heresy, harassment, and hypocrisy. We must arm ourselves with counter-defenses and keep them within reach at all times. Most of all, we must remember that "it was for freedom that Christ has set us free; therefore keep standing firm and do not be subject again to a yoke of slavery" (Galatians 5:1). The very truth of the gospel of grace is at stake.

Spreading Your Wings

These four powerful strategies will aid you in winning the inevitable conflict you'll encounter with legalism.

1. *Keep standing firm in your freedom.* Read Galatians 5:13–14; 22–25 and 1 Peter 2:15–17. How do Paul's and Peter's words—and the indwelling Holy Spirit—urge you to use your Christian freedom?

_____

2. *Stop seeking the favor of everyone.* Read Galatians 1:10. Paul warned believers not to become people pleasers who trade liberty for peace. He also condemned legalistic bullies, who force others to abide by their own standards. Are you leaning toward one of these extremes? If so, how can you avoid both of these, living out your own Christian freedom and allowing others to live out theirs?

_____

3. *Start refusing to submit to bondage.* Look again at Galatians 2:5. If there are people in your life now who are trying to enslave you in legalism, how can you wisely escape this trap while still demonstrating love to them?

_____

4. Think about your own views of the gospel. Do you believe you must do something to please God? Are any of your doctrinal beliefs robbing the gospel of its simple grace?

_____

5. *Continue being straightforward about the truth.* Read Galatians 2:14. If you act differently in your own home than in the company of your Christian friends, what can you do to avoid this hypocrisy?

_____

Anyone who is prone to use grace as a license
for irresponsible, sinful behavior, surely does not appreciate
the infinite price God paid
to give us His grace.
But anyone who tends to use legalism
as a hedge against license,
just as surely forgets
that grace cannot be earned
by our behavior.[7]

—JERRY BRIDGES

6

EMANCIPATED? THEN LIVE LIKE IT!

 Soaring on His Word

> *Therefore do not let sin reign in your mortal body so that you obey its lusts, and do not go on presenting the members of your body to sin as instruments of unrighteousness; but present yourselves to God as those alive from the dead, and your members as instruments of righteousness to God. For sin shall not be master over you, for you are not under law but under grace.*
>
> — ROMANS 6:12–14

JANUARY 1, 1863—the day the Emancipation Proclamation was legally adopted. Though headlines reading "Slavery Legally Abolished" swept from Capitol Hill to the valleys of Virginia into the Carolinas and across the plantations of Georgia, Alabama, Mississippi, and Louisiana, the great majority of the Southern slaves who were now legally freed continued to live in bondage. In fact, most continued living virtually unchanged lives throughout the Reconstruction period.

Shelby Foote records this anomaly in *The Civil War:*

> Locked into a caste system of "race etiquette" as rigid as any he had known in formal bondage . . . every slave could repeat with equal validity, what an Alabama slave had said in 1864 when asked what he thought of the Great Emancipator whose proclamation went into effect that year. "I don't know nothing bout Abraham Lincoln," he replied, "cep they say he sot us free. And I don't know nothing bout that neither."[1]

Though this man and numerous others like him had heard that Lincoln had set them free, they did not truly understand what their new freedom meant. So they continued living enslaved to men who were no longer their masters.

If a time machine took you back in time to talk to that Alabama slave who didn't "know nothing" about emancipation, what would you tell him about freedom?

_____

_____

_____

_____

How would you feel if you had to watch him continue living in slavery when you knew his freedom entitled him to experience a new life?

_____

_____

_____

_____

To our twenty-first-century ears, so accustomed to liberty, it sounds unbelievably tragic that legally freed people would actually choose to remain in bondage when they did not have to. Yet, many Christians today do the exact same thing in their spiritual lives. They embrace freedom with their words, but their actions show that they either don't understand what it means to be free or they fear their newfound freedom.

Rather than reaching out for the joys and risks liberty offers, many of us cling to the familiar "security" of spiritual slavery. And that's exactly what our old master, the devil, wants us to do. He uses every weapon in his arsenal to convince us that grace didn't really free us, that we're still guilty, and that we'll never be able to live without our old slave ways.

REVIEWING SOME THOUGHTS ON SPIRITUAL SLAVERY

In the book of Romans, Paul addressed the subject of spiritual slavery because he wanted us to understand that when Jesus died on the cross, He emancipated us from the devil's yoke of slavery. And that was no minor feat! The yoke of sin is a heavy weight.

All of us were born in bondage. Paul's words in Romans 3:10–20 show us that we were enslaved to sin. Symbolically, we were on the slave block, without hope and without excuse, depraved in ourselves, condemned by the Law, and completely unable to change our condition. Not one of us was righteous. Not one of us sought God. All of us turned aside.

A day came when our eternal Emancipator set us free. Our emancipation day occurred nearly 2000 years ago when Jesus gave His life for ours on a hill called Golgotha. He took the death sentence we deserved so that we could know God and enjoy a relationship with Him now and for eternity. According to Romans 3:24, we were "justified as a gift by His grace through the redemption which is in Christ Jesus." In other words, He saw us in our helpless condition and selflessly paid the price for our freedom. That grace freed us from our would-be master—sin.

Because of the Great Emancipator, we don't have to live under Master Sin anymore. We're free! Free to know God and free to follow Him, because His death satisfied the debt of death we owed for our sin. And, what's more, God raised Jesus from the dead, saying in effect, "No one need live under sin's reign any longer. All who believe in Jesus Christ, My Son, will have everlasting life and will have the power to live in Me." According to Romans 5:20–21, where sin once reigned, grace now "super-abounds."

Many of you may recall with misery your unsaved days. Remember how you couldn't get control of your desires? Perhaps you helplessly dropped into bed night after night a victim of a habit that you couldn't conquer for the life of you. You recall the feeling that there was no hope at the end of the tunnel—no light. No matter what, you could not change, not permanently. Remember how the shame increased and, at times, overwhelmed you? Or perhaps you've lived in the realm of freedom so long you've forgotten what it was like to be enslaved.

—The Grace Awakening

Many Christians who now have access to abounding grace still live as though they are enslaved. Sadly, just like the emancipated Alabama slave, these Christians say, "I don't know anything about grace except they say it set me free . . . and I don't know anything about that either."

You may say, "I've never said that I don't know anything about grace." But don't be so sure that you've never chanted the chain-wearers' mantra. It can come out in many different ways. Do any of these sound familiar to you? "You know, I . . . I just can't help myself." "Well, I'm only human." "Nobody's perfect." "God will forgive me later anyway." Our loyalty to our old master surfaces when we excuse our lustful thoughts, when we fudge on our income taxes, when we ignore the white lies we tell our mates, children, parents, employers, coworkers, and friends. All of these ignorant excuses and actions announce to the world, "I'm still enslaved. I'm choosing to go back to my old ways." And God's Word resounds back, "Where sin once abounded, grace now *superabounds!* Though you once were enslaved to your passions, you're now free from that. You can live above them!"

But Master Sin doesn't want you to live in freedom. He wants you to continue quivering in his presence, fearing his whip. He wants you to subject yourself to sin's beating on a regular basis, just to make you believe that you're not 100 percent free. Stop letting him whip you! You're free and you don't have to take his lashes anymore. You're not a slave. Sin's not your master anymore!

UNDERSTANDING THE FREEDOM GRACE BRINGS

Do you truly understand the freedom grace brought? Do you, therefore, live in liberty, or are you like the Alabama slave—still in bondage to one who is no longer your master? In Romans 6, Paul addressed two kinds of people who were spiritually emancipated but still living lives of slavery: grace nullifiers and grace abusers.

Read Romans 6:1–15. Consider the questions Paul asked in verses 1 and 15. Do you think these two questions are the same? Why or why not?

_____

_____

_____

_____

While these two questions may seem similar, they actually address two very different responses to grace. Verse 1 addresses *those who fail to claim their freedom and continue to live like slaves.* These people nullify grace because they continue to live in a state of sin. They're free, but they live like they're not. They choose to stay on their old master's plantation—to live, work, get whipped, and be miserable!

In contrast, verse 15 targets *those who take their freedom too far and take advantage of their liberty.* They live irresponsibly and abuse grace. They're free, but they choose to use their liberty to sin all the more. And to both the grace nullifiers and the grace abusers, Paul says, "No! Absolutely not. Don't live as though grace hasn't freed you, and don't sin as though real life comes through sinning!"

Before grace entered our lives, we didn't have the power to refuse sin. Our eyes led us to lust, our greed pushed us to fudge the numbers, and our fears let white lies keep us from truth. Our hearts were held captive by a malevolent master. And sometimes we still get caught up in his lies.

Describe below what your life was like before you came to Christ, when the malevolent master held your heart captive, or a time in your Christian walk when you felt powerless to break free from his chains.

_____

_____

_____

_____

If you have been freed from his captivity, why do you sometimes choose to continue living as if you were still enslaved?

_____

_____

_____

_____

If we're not careful, we find ourselves returning to slavery because we know how to be slaves. Though we don't like the bondage, we do like the familiar security of our old ways. We've learned negative patterns that give us certain results. Living as slaves seems less risky than testing our newfound liberty. We don't think we're strong enough to live in freedom so we willingly return to our chains. When we doubt our strength, we're actually refusing to draw on God's power to enable us to say no to sin. We haven't learned that our victory comes from Him rather than us. With Christ, it's not impossible to resist sin. It's not beyond our control. We've just been programmed to think that it is!

Look up 1 John 1:9 and write it below.

_____

_____

_____

_____

Now, turn to Romans 6:13 and write it below.

_____

_____

_____

_____

First John 1:9 tells us what to do when we have sinned. Romans 6:13 tells us what to do to resist the sin patterns that we're accustomed to following.

Do you lean on the truth of Romans 6:13 as much as you trust the teaching of 1 John 1:9? Why do most of us find it easier to fail and be forgiven rather than to yield ourselves to God *before* we fail?

_____

_____

_____

_____

Let's stop saying, "Yes, Master," to sin and start saying, "Lord Jesus Christ, this is Your day, to be lived for Your glory. Work through my eyes, my ears, my mouth, and my actions to carry out Your victory all day long." Yes, we will fail at times. But we won't live in a continual state of failure if we run quickly from the old master and return to our true Master. The continual desire to be free from our former master allows us to yield to sin less and less and yield to God more and more.

CLAIMING VICTORY OVER SIN

Remember that Master Sin, or the old sinful nature that once ruled over us, has been removed from power. But, the devil doesn't like that he's lost his power over us, so he does everything he can to convince us to continue giving in to sin. Since we're now under grace, we can and must counteract sin's power. The obvious question is, how? While it's easy to pay lip service to resisting sin, it's much harder to actually do it!

What can we do to keep our old master out of control? Paul presented three practical applications in Romans 6. He advised that to walk in freedom from the old master and experience the liberty of our new lives, we must "know" some things (6:3), "consider" something (6:11), and "present" something (6:13).

Know

What do we need to know? Read Romans 6:3–8. Verse 3 tells us "that all of us who have been baptized into Christ Jesus have been baptized into His death." Paul wasn't talking about water baptism here. Rather, he was talking about a spiritual baptism. Just as the Israelites "were baptized into Moses in the cloud and in the sea" (1 Corinthians 10:2), everyone who believes in Jesus is spiritually immersed in Him.

FLYING AGAINST THE WINDS OF OUR CULTURE

Are you ready for a maverick thought? Once we truly grasp the freedom grace brings, we can resist sinning or feeling ashamed. We really can! And why not? Why should sin gain mastery over us? Who says we cannot help but yield to it? How unbiblical! You see, most of us are so programmed to sin that we wait for it to happen. We're convinced that it's inevitable. Why don't we fight it? What in the world has happened to our message of victory in Christ? Why in the world was He raised from the dead? Not just to give us forgiveness, but to give us victory!

GETTING TO THE ROOT

The Greek word *baptizo* wasn't a religious term. It simply meant to "immerse." To *baptizo* a white garment into purple dye was to immerse it in the dye. The word could also imply identification with a substance. For example, the white garment dipped in purple dye became like the dye it was dipped into—purple.

The moment we believed that Christ died for us on the cross and was raised from the dead in the tomb, we too were "baptized," immersed in Christ. What does that mean to us personally? It means that we have been set free from sin, because what died on the cross with Christ was what Paul called our "old man." The spiritual person we were before coming to Christ—the "us" that was born in Adam (see Romans 5:12–21), the rebel opposed to God and enslaved to sin—died. And when he (or she) died, the chain that sin had around us was broken. We were raised with Christ as new creations (2 Corinthians 5:17) over whom sin had lost its power—free now to love, obey, and be in relationship with God. And, being joined to Christ, we now have One living in us who always "lives to God" (Romans 6:10). His life is our life. His victory is our victory. His freedom is our freedom.

Look at Romans 6:6–7. If Christ's death set you free and He lives in you, are you free from sin's control in every way? How does this truth affect your day-to-day life?

_____

_____

_____

Romans 6:8–10 affirms that just as we died with Christ, we will also live with Him. We are joined to Him, and we have all the power we need to live above the level of slavery that bound us in our past lives. Our new life is resurrection life with Christ. We have been given victory!

Victory begins in knowing that all who believe in Christ are spiritually free. We need to focus our minds on the truths that remind us why we who believe in Christ are free:

- We were joined to Christ in His death and resurrection.
- Our "old man," inherited from Adam, died with Him, breaking sin's power over us.

- Jesus Himself now lives in us, and we are recipients of His power.
- All of this is ours—right now!

Consider

Now that we know we are united with Christ in both His death and His resurrection, that we are recipients of His power, and that His power has freed us from the old master, we need to consider some things.

Romans 6:11 tells us to consider ourselves "dead to sin, but alive to God in Christ Jesus." Being in Christ, we are dead to sin's power. And we are alive with God's power.

Since we are dead to sin's power and alive with God's power, we have the power to say no to sin. Romans 6:12 commands us to deny sin's reign in our mortal bodies, to say no to its lusts, to kick the old master out of the place he no longer reigns. Our bodies, which once belonged to him, are his no longer. So why do we continue acting as if they are? Even though we can now say no to sin, often we still say yes. That's why Romans 6:13 commands us to change our ways: "Do not go on presenting the members of your body to sin."

Present

Not only are we to intelligently consider our freedom in Christ based upon what we know, we are to consciously *present* the members of our bodies to God for His use. Romans 6:13 tells us to do this in two ways. First, we're to stop presenting the members of our bodies to unrighteousness. And second, in the very moment that the attack occurs, we're to turn to God's power that is within us, surrender the battle to God, and say no to sin and yes to righteousness.

A REALISTIC WARNING

Just because we're free doesn't mean it's easy to say no to sin. Our struggle against sin will at times seem too great to bear. But, if we draw on God's power to say no to sin and yes to righteousness, we will be victorious. It will work!

Spreading Your Wings

The next time you are tempted to put the chains back on your wrists and follow your old master, what will you do?

Think of a certain sin that you often give in to. What do you now *know* that will help you say no to this sin?

_____

_____

_____

_____

What do you need to *consider* in order to say yes to righteousness?

_____

_____

_____

How can you *present* yourself to righteousness rather than to sin in this specific issue?

_____

_____

_____

_____

*Regenerate Christians should no more contemplate
a return to unregenerate living than adults to their childhood,
married people to their singleness, or discharged prisoners
to their prison cell. For our union with Jesus Christ
has severed us from the old life
and committed us to the new. . . .
We have died, and we have risen.
How can we possibly live again
in what we have died to?*[2]

—JOHN STOTT

7

GUIDING OTHERS TO FREEDOM

 Soaring on His Word

Do you not know that when you present yourselves to some-one as slaves for obedience, you are slaves of the one whom you obey, either of sin resulting in death, or of obedience resulting in righteousness?

—ROMANS 6:16

IKE THE SLAVE from Alabama in the sad story told in the previous chapter, every Christian remembers what it was like to be held captive by the old master, sin. Before Christ freed us from sin's bondage, we were locked into a life we couldn't escape on our own. We needed a liberator to free us.

Jesus was that Emancipator. While we rejoice that His sacrifice brought us liberty from the penalty, guilt, shame, and power of sin, we often fail to use our freedom in Christ for its intended purpose. In addition, we often refuse to extend to others the liberty He gives us. It's as if we're former Southern slaves who "do know something about Abraham Lincoln—that he sot us free," but instead of bandaging the fingers of our freed brothers and sisters and leading them to a life of joyful service under our new, loving Master, we tell them to keep picking cotton.

We sometimes lead others back to another part of the same plantation, believing we're still under the power of sin and failing to embrace our new freedom. At other times, we submit ourselves and others to a taskmaster called legalism, which did nothing to free us from our former bondage of sin. Some believers acknowledge their freedom from the requirements of the law and legalism, but fail to fully embrace the righteousness of Christ.

Our job is to free people; God's job is to restrain them. God is doing his job much better than we are doing ours.

—The Grace Awakening

We who have been freed by Christ must avoid taking the role of the legalistic taskmaster or the deceptive abuser of license, which are really two forms of the power of sin and death. Instead, our goal as Christians should be to understand and walk in our own freedom through the power of the Holy Spirit, submitting to the lordship of Christ, who alone deserves our allegiance.

Such a life of righteousness is not a constraint we place on ourselves to earn God's approval or on others to try to influence the way they live their lives. This would interfere with Christ's lordship in the life of individual believers through the Holy Spirit. Instead, we should be encouraged—and encourage others—to embrace the freedom we have in Christ, discover the balance between self-restraint and liberty, and wisely use our freedom to serve Him.

Why do you think many Christians find restricting others' freedom easier than releasing others to find their own balance between self-restraint and liberty in the service of Christ?

_____

_____

_____

_____

WONDERFUL TRUTHS REGARDING FREEDOM

Scripture encourages us again and again to embrace freedom. Read the following verses aloud, and let their liberating words remind you that you are truly free, once and for all:

It was for freedom that Christ set us free. (Galatians 5:1)

He who has died is freed from sin. (Romans 6:7)

For the law of the Spirit of life in Christ Jesus has set you free. (Romans 8:2)

And you will know the truth, and the truth will make you free. (John 8:32)

So if the Son makes you free, you will be free indeed. (John 8:36)

These verses assure us of our eternal life and our freedom to resist sin as we live in a world system that's still under its dominion. But, as we battle the pressures and temptations of the world, we can be tempted to put on our "no" faces and forget to enjoy the freedom we have. We're presented with a choice regarding our freedom: either to use it in bondage to sin in the forms of legalism or license, or to use it to serve Christ through the power of the Spirit.

Given these choices, we may be tempted to deny freedom and take the road of legalism, forming a long list of dos and don'ts that we cram down the throats of others. But we must resist this temptation as we would any other sin! Instead, we're called to take hold of our Christian liberty as Paul instructed the Corinthians to do.

Read 1 Corinthians 10:23–30. What was the problem in the Corinthian butcher shops?

_____

_____

_____

_____

How did Paul's advice to the Corinthians allow them to stop focusing on restrictions and start discovering their freedom in Christ? What were the drawbacks of this shift in thinking? The benefits?

_____

_____

_____

_____

WINDOWS TO THE ANCIENT WORLD

In first-century Corinth, some Christians had a beef about meat and were clucking their tongues about it. In ancient pagan worship, portions of meat were offered to idols, and the rest of the animal was often sold in a meat market. Some people refused to eat the leftover meat because they considered it to be contaminated.[1] After all, if part of it had been offered to idols, all of it must have been tainted, right? But Paul responded, "Eat anything that is sold in the meat market without asking questions for conscience' sake; for the earth is the Lord's, and all it contains" (1 Corinthians 10:25).

Whether or not the meat was offered to idols, God considered it clean because He had set His people free from the former strict dietary codes and rules. Paul wanted believers to stop focusing on food and start focusing on freedom, as long as their liberty didn't cause other people to stumble.

The Corinthians focused on meat when Paul wanted them to focus on ministry. The apostle exhorted these believers to eat freely, as long as the exercise of their freedom didn't offend a weaker brother. Likewise, he admonished those who still didn't feel the freedom to eat the meat not to slander their brothers and sisters who chose to eat it.

Most twenty-first-century Christians don't grapple with the issue of eating meat offered to idols, but sometimes we argue about "gray areas"—issues that Scripture does not specifically mention or classify as right or wrong. Our divisive arguments can overshadow what's truly important—living in loving harmony with our fellow believers and leading non-Christians to a knowledge of Christ.

What a great life mission we have! We're called to help people cut the chains that keep them from embracing their freedom from sin to live lives of righteousness. We're encouraged to remove the veil that clouds their view of the way they experience liberty. Following Paul's example, let's lead others to discover lavish grace rather than languishing grace.

Read 1 Timothy 6:17. Do you spend your days enjoying God's provision and encouraging other Christians to do the same? Take a moment to be honest with yourself. In the past six months, how have you enjoyed your own freedom in Christ or helped a brother or sister discover the depths of his or her freedom?

_____

_____

_____

_____

Do you ever let your convictions on the gray issues restrain your freedom so much that it keeps you from accepting an unbeliever's hospitality or friendship? If so, how?

_____

_____

_____

_____

Have you ever slandered a fellow believer who exercised freedom in a gray area where you practiced restraint? Consider the following scenarios:

- Looking down on your neighbors from "that other church" who have a glass of wine with dinner
- Scoffing when someone mentions watching a TV show you would never watch
- Feeling more godly because your children attend Christian school or are homeschooled
- Talking about the couples from your church who went dancing at a nightclub last Saturday night
- Feeling superior to the people who just used their tax refund to put a down payment on a BMW, since you donated your tax refund to the missions fund

Arguments about issues such as these can cause problems within families, divide churches, and destroy lives. We needn't split hairs about things that Scripture doesn't condemn.

On the other hand, what if the issue we're facing isn't gray at all? What if it's clearly addressed in Scripture, and we see a brother or sister going against it? Then, we're not dealing with a list of preferences. Instead, we're dealing with God's list of commands. But before we go hit our brother or sister over the head with our Bibles, we need to ask ourselves some questions.

God has given His children a wonderful freedom in Christ, which means not only freedom from sin and shame but also freedom in lifestyle so that we can become models of His grace.
—The Grace Awakening

First, is the person clearly contradicting a scriptural command that applies to life today? Second, are we following God's Word faithfully ourselves? Before we scrutinize the actions of others, we need to closely examine our own faithfulness. And third, is our motive in talking to our brother or sister one of love or judgment? If we're approaching the person out of love, we need to pray first and talk second. Though we may struggle to confront him or her in a loving manner, our message is more likely to be received if we do so. If we approach the person with an attitude of condemnation or harsh judgment, we might as well not go. Few people will respond to our attempts to pound truth into their heads using a two-by-four! Most of us can't think very clearly after sustaining a concussion.

In order to be the creatures God has made us to be, we need to listen more to Him and less to others. That's hard to do if we're insecure. If you were raised in an environment in which you were urged to be a people pleaser, it may take years for you to learn how to walk freely in the grace of God, trusting in *Him* for direction rather than relying on a man-made list of rules. On the other hand, if such an upbringing left you as a grace abuser who tends to overstep the bounds of self-restraint and abuse liberty, you face the challenge of learning how to enjoy grace's freedom without cheapening it. As tragic as it is when believers fail to embrace liberating grace, it's even more devastating when we use our freedom as a license for recklessness. It's this use of freedom, balanced with God's restraint, that we need to address further.

Two Questions that Make Us Think

To discover how to walk in grace without overstepping its bounds, let's return to the two questions from Romans 6 that we addressed in the previous chapter.

We said that Romans 6:1 addresses those who fail to claim their freedom and continue to live like slaves. These believers are so convinced that sin's going to get them that they "speed dial" God every day, pleading for forgiveness for the sins they have just committed rather than claiming Christ's victorious power over their habitual sin. This type of person, rather than avoiding the "crash" of sin altogether, would rather rely on the Great Paramedic to fix him or her up after the fact.

Romans 6:15 targets those individuals who take their freedom too far and take advantage of their liberty. These folks think that grace is a license to live irresponsibly. They cruise straight for the hazardous traffic of sin because they assume they have a blanket insurance policy that allows them to own the road. Some go so far as driving the wrong way down the streets Scripture has clearly marked "One Way." They believe, "Extramarital affair? No problem—grace will cover it!" "Cheating on taxes? God wouldn't mind, would He?" These believers seem to forget that twisting Scripture to accommodate their desires has nothing to do with grace!

Paul knew that grace abusers would misunderstand the intent of Christ's sacrifice, so he gave us some warnings about how to handle our free yet priceless grace with care.

Careful Warnings To All Who Are Free

Because we're free (and we are free, indeed!), we have a choice. Romans 6:16 presents us with the choice that we as Christians face each day: Which master will we choose to serve?

As you consider the decisions you've made in the last three days, do your choices reveal an obedience to your old master, sin, or your new Master, Christ?

_____

_____

_____

Here's the heart of verse 16: How we live depends on the master we choose. Obeying a master means enslaving yourself to that master. Verses 17–19 remind us that in our past condition, we were enslaved to sin—we had no alternative but to serve it, and our appetite for sin only grew worse. But, after Jesus freed us, we changed masters. In our newfound freedom, we have the choice to chain ourselves to sin or to tie ourselves to righteousness.

Verses 19–21 exhort us to make the right choice! God loves us so much that He sends us, his liberated children, out into a world where we can choose to pursue "sin that results in death" or "obedience that leads to righteousness." Before we knew God, we had no choice but to pursue sin that led to death. We were powerless against lust, jealousy, selfishness, and the rest of sin's horrific list. But now, we can choose to follow Christ or to return to sin. We're free from the requirement to obey sin, and we're free to voluntarily follow Christ's leadership and avoid sin!

But the opposite is also true: if we say no to Christ as our Master, we say yes to sin, whether it means serving the taskmaster of legalism or the loose lifestyle of license. The spiritual principle seems simple, but its application can be difficult. It's quite possible for us to sin far less than we do, but the world in which we live and the flesh with which we're bound make it impossible for us to be perfect and sinless on this earth. Nevertheless, we have a choice to make between two very different masters. Which will you choose to serve?

Though we know better, we sometimes choose to follow our flesh and fall back into the old habits we knew when sin was our master. In His grace, God allows us freedom, but if we continually choose to use our freedom wrongly, we adopt a lifestyle that becomes increasingly more sinful.

Consider the message of Proverbs 5:21–23 by putting your name in the blanks:

For the ways of _____ are before the eyes of the LORD,
And He watches all _____'s paths.
_____'s own iniquities will capture _____,
And _____ will be held with the cords of his [her] sin.
_____ will die for lack of instruction,
And in the greatness of _____'s folly he [she] will go astray.

Though we picture this proverb as an address to unbelievers, it's also a warning to believers about the whirlpool of wickedness that threatens to drown us when we follow sin. If we continue in that sin, we become less willing to fight against it and more likely to let it rob us of the air of freedom we breathe. While we are free to follow sin's pull, we'll face the consequences of its undertow, including the most serious one—grieving our heavenly Father.

FLYING AGAINST THE WINDS OF OUR CULTURE

Addiction has become a buzzword in the twenty-first century, whether it's a penchant for overeating, chain-smoking, alcoholism, too much caffeine, soap operas, pornography, 24/7 sports, drugs, or overwork. Everyone faces the snare of such addictions. The world calls addiction a disease, but the Bible calls it carnality.

Once we choose to become believers, the Holy Spirit empowers us to say no to temptations that can grow into addictions. But if we choose not to access His power and we continue in habitual sin, we risk losing our way and our witness. Don't make the mistake of living carnally and excusing it by claiming grace.

If you find yourself addicted to certain sins, you can break the shackles.

- Make the decision to stop your habitual sin and trust in Christ's power to follow through.

- Bring your sin out in the open with select accountability partners you can trust; hidden sin makes you more vulnerable to addiction.

- Pray for release from your habit of sin and ask your accountability partners to pray for you.

- Give a friend or group of friends permission to ask you tough questions about your life.

- Keep your answers honest—lying stunts life change!

Spreading Your Wings

Read Colossians 1:9–12. In Paul's prayer for the Colossians, what was the source of power that motivated these believers' godly lifestyle?

_____

_____

_____

_____

Looking back over the past week of your life, what's been the motivation for the choices you've made?

_____

_____

_____

_____

Our attitudes and actions tend to follow the focus of our hearts. What's your top priority or primary goal today: serving self, others, or Christ? What does this reveal about which master you're truly following?

_____

_____

_____

_____

Sin, the illegitimate master, pays us in death wages. If we follow him, he'll lead us to a breakdown in fellowship with God, the misery of a guilty conscience, the loss of our personal testimony and integrity, and the stunting of our growth as Christians.

Thankfully, Jesus's death and resurrection freed us from sin's mastery. It also provided us with access to God—our righteous Master—and opened the door to the exciting process of maturing in Christ, living guilt-free to pursue life with passion and creativity, and one day enjoying eternal life in heaven. Our old master, sin, bound us in death, but our new Master freed us to enjoy abundant life on earth and everlasting life in heaven! Refuse to be held captive by sin. Embrace your freedom and encourage your freed brothers and sisters to do the same!

Sin begets sin. The first time we do a wrong thing,
we may do it with hesitation, and a tremor and a shudder.
The second time we do it, it is easier and if we keep on doing it,
it becomes effortless; sin loses its terror. . . .
To start on the path of sin
is to go on to more and more. [2]

—WILLIAM BARCLAY

8

THE GRACE TO LET OTHERS BE

 Soaring on His Word

Therefore let us not judge one another anymore, but rather determine this—not to put an obstacle or a stumbling block in a brother's way. . . . So then let us pursue the things which make for peace and the building up of one another.
—ROMANS 14:13, 19

Have you ever felt the pressure of being stuck under someone else's microscope? Whether it was your parents, siblings, teachers, or well-meaning friends who scrutinized your behavior, you probably know what it feels like to fall short of someone else's standard. Those who peer at us through a narrow lens of judgment often magnify our shortcomings—asserting their ideals as being the ultimate way to please God. And therein lies the error of their theology! We don't earn our righteousness before God at salvation, and we don't have to do anything after we are saved to earn God's approval as we live our lives on earth. He is pleased with us because of what Jesus did on the cross. When Jesus died on that tree, He imparted right standing before God to all who would believe in Him. Every believer's standing before God comes only from grace.

So why do so many people who have received a grace they did nothing to deserve continue to withhold it from others? Most likely, they don't mean to be grace killers. The majority of them do it because they don't understand that grace exists both on a vertical level with God and on a horizontal level with other people.

The vertical grace—the grace that God holds out to sinners—truly is amazing. It frees us from the demands of the law. It offers us God's very own righteousness as our own. It imparts to us His very own life.

Grace on the horizontal plane—grace that gives others room to breathe—can't bring eternal salvation, but it is amazing in its own way. It, too, originates with God; it's only by receiving His grace that we have grace to offer others. Horizontal grace liberates people from the demands of one another's expectations and guilt-driven manipulations. It also frees us from the clutches of our own self-critical consciences.

Stop and remember a time when someone put you under a microscope. List five words that describe the way you reacted when your freedom was squashed.

_____

_____

_____

_____

Now, consider a tougher question: have you ever squashed someone else's freedom? Are you doing so now? You may need to think about the various people in your life and ask, "How do I, overtly or subtly, communicate my shoulds and my should nots to them?"

_____

_____

_____

_____

What we really believe shows through in the expectations we put on others. We can offer mercy to others or give them no mercy. The grace giver's accepting attitude liberates. The grace killer's rigid attitude restricts. Every day, we choose whether our attitude will bring others hope or guilt. As you read the words of Auschwitz survivor Viktor Frankl, consider how the right attitude can bring light into the darkest circumstances:

> We who lived in concentration camps can remember the men who walked through the huts comforting others, giving away their last piece of bread. They may have been few in number, but they offer sufficient proof that

everything can be taken from a man but one thing: the last of the human freedoms—to choose one's attitude in any given set of circumstances. . . .

And there were always choices to make. Every day, every hour, offered the opportunity to make a decision . . . which determined whether you would or would not submit to those powers which threatened to rob you of your very self, your inner freedom; which determined whether or not you would become the plaything of circumstance, renouncing freedom and dignity to become molded into the form of the typical inmate. . . .

. . . Even though conditions such as lack of sleep, insufficient food and various mental stresses may suggest that the inmates were bound to react in certain ways, in the final analysis it becomes clear that the sort of person the prisoner became was the result of an inner decision, and not the result of camp influences alone.[1]

Our attitude makes a difference! Regardless of our circumstances, we can choose to treat people with dignity.

Chances are that all of us have stepped into legalism and on someone else's freedom at one time or another. It's easy to do. Sometimes we mean to do it. Other times, we do it out of our own broken backgrounds or misguided intentions. Whatever our reasons for restricting others' freedom, we need to stop trying to control them and instead release them to be the people God directs them to be.

So how do we do this? The process starts, not by focusing on their behavior, but by examining the motives of our own hearts. How we treat our brothers and sisters begins with our view of God. Do we truly believe that He's big enough not only to allow but to encourage diversity within the body of believers? Or do we think God needs our help to ensure the quality control of His children? Before we answer too quickly with the obviously correct choice, let's take some time to really consider our true tendencies.

Two Strong Tendencies That Nullify Grace: Controlling and Comparing

In Romans 12:9–18, read Paul's very practical admonishment to live authentically by loving our Christian brothers and sisters well.

After reading these words, we're all sure to say a big, "Amen!" After all, that's what

FLYING AGAINST THE WINDS OF OUR CULTURE

Consider the true story of the Christian college student who encountered a fellow student who wasn't interested in becoming a Christian. When she asked why and pressed the issue a little further, he answered her, "Because the most guilt-ridden people I know are Christians. No, thanks."

Ironic, isn't it? Some of us—the very people whose guilt and shame have been erased by the grace of the Savior—tend to carry the burden of blame with every step we take. Why? Because we tend to be people who don't embrace grace for ourselves or hold it out to others. Sure, we believe that grace gives us eternal life, but we're not absolutely certain that it frees us in the here and now. What a warped message this guilt-based living sends to the unbelievers in our circles!

---

it's like to be a part of the family of God. Right? The church isn't a place filled with hypocrites who love evil more that good. It's a place where one person willingly puts another's needs ahead of his or her own and blesses those who don't respond in the same way. A place we can celebrate our joys without worrying that the Joneses will be jealous of our good fortune. A place where people share our tears without trying to wipe them away with a cliché and a Bible verse. Right? Sadly, most of us would have to say, "Wrong!" because we don't find such a place when we walk through the doors of our churches on Sunday mornings.

Why have so many of the church bodies that are supposedly filled with Romans 12:9–18 people turned into the most unsafe places? It's because we tend to focus on ourselves and forget about each other. In this self-focused state, we seek to compare ourselves with other people. When we size ourselves up as better than others, we criticize them. When we think we're inferior to them, we covet their position and compete with them. When we indulge in self-centered choices rather than God-centered living, we seek to control others in an effort to bolster our own fragile self-images. These two strong tendencies, *comparing* and *controlling*, nullify grace.

Comparing Ourselves with Others

Why do we so often think that being Christians means being alike? We tend to view those who are different from us with suspicion rather than with acceptance. We act as though the church is a factory in the business of turning out assembly-line people. But God's not an automaker whose standard demands that every one of us look the same and respond the same way to a situation. While that's great quality control for Ford, Chevrolet, Honda, and Toyota, it's stifling control that God never intended His church to impose on His children. In God's economy, sameness is suspect. Variety honors God. Christ makes us all different so we might add diversity, beauty, and substance to the body. Our differences can inspire and motivate us, as well as break down the boredom that often creeps into the family of God.

Do you give a fellow Christ-follower the freedom to be completely different from you (and still be your friend), or does embracing variety within the body of Christ scare you?

_____

_____

_____

_____

Before you answer too quickly, consider this:

Would you be comfortable worshiping with the following people: A murderer? An adulterer? A slick businessman who got rich by taking your neighbors' hard-earned money? A rough-around-the-edges woman who made her living on the street before she joined your Wednesday night prayer service? A person whose attire makes him or her look odd or someone who smells funny to you? An outspoken political activist whose views differ from your own? An immigrant from a foreign country that warred against your own?

Moses, David, and the apostle Paul all had murder on their rap sheets. David also committed adultery. When Jesus invited him into fellowship, Matthew was a tax collector who got rich off the poor. Rahab, the woman who helped the Israelite spies escape from Jericho and the great, great, great grandmother of David, was a prostitute. The woman who anointed Jesus's feet with perfume was too. John the Baptist's camelhaired apparel and locust diet surely made him look odd and smell funny. Cornelius's diet initially turned Peter's stomach. Simon the Zealot was on the left side of Jerusalem's political scene when Jesus called him to be a disciple. (Keep in mind that he served Jesus alongside Matthew, the man who once worked for the very causes he had opposed.) Ruth was a foreigner from Moab who sought and found refuge and relationship with the people who hated her countrymen.

List some modern-day equivalents to these Old and New Testament people of faith who might be met with restrictive guidelines rather than charming grace if they joined or visited your church.

_____

_____

_____

_____

Controlling Others

Living in grace implies that we are committed to letting people go. We release our right (which is really not our right at all) to give them an agenda or put them under an unrealistic load of expectations. It means letting them grow at the rate and in the manner God determines. It doesn't imply that we can't challenge them to change in areas where they have clearly stepped over scriptural boundaries. But it does mean we'd better be sure that the line they've crossed isn't a gray one. When we're certain it is truly black and white, we need to approach them with grace rather than overwhelming them with rules.

Consider the way Nathan approached David in 2 Samuel 12:1–15 after discovering the king had murdered his employee to cover up his adultery. Recall how Jesus drew Peter with love in John 21:15–17 after Peter had abandoned and denied Him. Both Nathan and Jesus challenged the men they confronted to change without using guilt to manipulate them or guidelines to control them. When you find yourself wanting to control others, you know you've made the mistake of holding on to people too tightly and too quickly letting go of grace.

FOUR BIBLICAL GUIDELINES THAT RELEASE OTHERS TO GROW UNDER GRACE

In Romans 14, Paul addressed the issue of personal freedom in great detail so that we would understand how to give others horizontal grace by releasing them from our expectations and encouraging them to grow under God's grace.

Read Romans 14:1–4. Remember that early Christians struggled with whether or not they should eat meat from the carcass of an animal that had been offered to idols. Paul's advice to the Christians of that day still applies to Christians of our day. He basically said, "Let the one whose faith is weaker skip the meat and enjoy veggie shish-kabobs. And let the one who has faith to eat all things savor meat—unless the meat-eater's freedom causes the greens-eater to struggle. And, finally, let neither one judge the other."

Now that we've looked at some actions and attitudes that can nullify grace, let's discover four guidelines that release grace.

Guideline 1: Accepting others is basic to letting them be. The absence of judgment makes room for an acceptance motivated by love. Though today we're not debating over round steak versus rack of lamb, we do tend to turn the fire on high when we're not comfortable with a fellow believer's choices. Consider the following hot topics:

- Does the use of birth control take life out of God's control?
- To tattoo or not tattoo—that is the question.
- Pierced ears . . . Pierced noses . . . Pierced belly buttons?
- Is a person who has had cosmetic surgery only skin deep?
- Contemporary worship music versus traditional hymns versus meeting in the middle.
- Wine (alcohol) with dinner? Coffee (caffeine) with breakfast?
- Bathing suits: two pieces or one?
- Dual-income families versus Mom or Dad staying home.
- When is dancing dirty, and when is it good, clean fun?
- Can an elegant home be too opulent?
- Can physical fitness become self-absorption?
- Does all work and no play mean Jack or Jill is industrious, or obsessed?
- When does keeping pace with the traffic turn into breaking the speed limit?

Before you burn another believer by imposing your convictions on them or by leading them astray with liberties they're not free to enjoy, ask yourself how you would want someone on the other side of the thin gray line to treat you, and act accordingly.

Look at Romans 14:5–8. What should determine a person's conviction on a gray issue?

_____

_____

_____

_____

Guideline 2: Refusing to dictate to others allows the Lord freedom to direct their lives. Just as good parents allow each of their children to grow up at their own speed with safe boundaries that leave them room to explore, more spiritually mature Christians need to allow less mature believers to pursue various roads toward maturity at their own pace—even when the paths they choose lead to failure.

Consider the lessons Abraham, Sarah, Isaac, Jacob, David, Martha, and Peter each learned from failure. Consider the lessons you have learned from failure. In His grace, God allows us to fail and grows us through our failures. Let's give others the same grace.

Move on to Romans 14:9–12. These words leave us awed and humbled.

Guideline 3: Freeing others means we never assume a position we're not qualified to fill. We don't judge each other. We should marvel that the One who is our Judge sent his Son to take the death sentence we deserved. We should fall on our faces before we have the audacity to judge another brother or sister who—like us—has been rescued from death row.

Place an X by the statements that prevent you from being qualified to judge others:

____I don't know all the facts.

____I can't read motives perfectly.

____I can never be 100 percent objective.

____I can't see the big picture.

___I have blind spots.

___My prejudices blur my perspective.

___I am imperfect and inconsistent.

Choosing not to judge doesn't mean that we must agree with our brothers' or sisters' decisions. It does call us to reign in our assumptions, weigh our thoughts, and hold our tongues on matters that aren't ours to measure.

Now, read Romans 14:13–18. The first of these six verses admonishes us to stop judging others and start considering their welfare as more important than our own. The question isn't who's right. Rather, it's what's more important—your liberty or the well-being of your Christian brothers and sisters?

Guideline 4: Loving others requires us to express our liberty wisely. A person marked with maturity exercises liberty without flaunting it. Grace never gives us the right to rub anyone's nose in our liberty.

A Few Actions that Signify Grace

What can we do to make sure that we are extending grace to one another? Here are four steps that will keep us on the path of grace.

1. *Concentrate on things that encourage peace and assist others' growth.* Paul says this in Romans 14:19. Before you speak, ask yourself, *Will this build up or tear down? Will this contribute to peace or disunity?*

2. *Remember that sabotaging saints hurts the work of God.* Romans 14:20 calls us "the work of God." God doesn't want His own handiwork undone.

3. *Exercise your liberty only with those who can enjoy it with you.* If it's a gray issue that's okay for you and okay for a friend, have a great time. If it's not okay for a friend, restrain yourself out of love and respect for him or her.

4. *Determine where you stand, and refuse to "play God" in anyone else's life.* Be firm about your own convictions, but don't demand that others follow them when God doesn't demand it.

Spreading Your Wings

Philippians 2:3–4 captures the spirit of Romans 14 in a single charge: "Do nothing from selfishness or empty conceit, but with humility of mind, regard one another as more important than yourselves; do not merely look out for your own personal interests, but also for the interests of others."

Do you ever look down on your brothers and sisters who don't share your convictions? If so, what motivates your attitude?

_____

_____

_____

_____

Do you sometimes exercise your liberty without considering how your choice will affect a weaker brother or sister? Who are you putting first when you do this?

_____

_____

_____

_____

Let's change the trend. Let's focus less on exercising our own desires and more on loving others. Let's care less about making others like ourselves and more about extending the grace that helps others be who God wants them to be. Let's spend less time considering how we might change others and more time considering how God delights in them as His children. Let's give others the grace that God has given to us.

My study of Jesus's life convinces me that whatever barriers
we must overcome in treating "different" people
cannot compare to what a holy God—who dwelled in the Most Holy Place,
and whose presence caused fire and smoke to belch from mountaintops,
bringing death to any unclean person who wandered near—
overcame when he descended to join us on planet Earth.[2]

—PHILIP YANCEY

9
GRACIOUSLY DISAGREEING AND PRESSING ON

 Soaring on His Word

Let no unwholesome word proceed from your mouth, but only such a word as is good for edification according to the need of the moment, so that it will give grace to those who hear.

— EPHESIANS 4:29

WHEN IT COMES TO DISAGREEMENTS, are you a lover or a fighter? Do you attempt to make peace, or do you throw punches and go for a knockout in the first round? Do you patiently put up with disagreements, or do you immediately "put up your dukes" when faced with conflict?

Some of us are real fighters who thrive on disagreement and debate. We may salivate at the chance to beat somebody over the head with facts, rip them to pieces with words, or intimidate them with other battle tactics. Others of us can be more subtle but just as mean. When we disagree with others, we may manipulate them, make them feel guilty, or give them the silent treatment, forcing them to drop to their knees and beg for forgiveness.

While being a verbal heavyweight or a mastermind of manipulation may help contestants win reality TV shows, these abilities don't serve us well where it really counts—in God's kingdom. From God's perspective, it's not whether you win or lose; it's how you play the game. Whether the issue is where to send missions money or what color to paint the church nursery, God doesn't care nearly as much about the decision as He does about the process of deciding. In His eyes, those who "win" are those who learn to show grace to others, regardless of what final decision is made. We win when we are transformed into Christ's likeness, not when we stubbornly demand our own way. The inevitable disagreements in life provide fertile soil for our spiritual growth.

One of the marks of Christian maturity is the ability to disagree without becoming disagreeable, yet few of us are consistently grace-oriented in our disagreements. Most of us have plenty of room for growth in this area.

How do you tend to respond when faced with a disagreement—are you a fighter, a manipulator, one who avoids conflict, or one who handles conflict with grace?

_____

_____

_____

_____

THINGS WE AGREE ON REGARDING DISAGREEMENTS

Despite our differences, we can agree on the following principles regarding disagreements.

1. *Disagreements are inevitable.* Ever since the first disagreement over whose fault it was that Adam and Eve ate the forbidden fruit (Genesis 3:11–13), disagreements and differences of opinion have been constant realities. Because individuals have unique perspectives, experiences, tastes, and personalities, they will take opposing viewpoints on many issues. Acknowledging and expecting disagreements is the first step to approaching them with grace.

2. *Even the godly will disagree.* Doesn't being mature, godly, and Spirit-filled mean we will always agree? Won't God lead us to a consensus when we're walking with Him? Sometimes, yes; sometimes, no. God's will may be worked out in a community of believers through our disagreement as well as through our agreement. In His sovereign power and wisdom, God uses people who disagree with each other from time to time. We must accept that disagreements will occur even among born-again, mature believers.

3. *Every disagreement contains two ingredients: an issue and various viewpoints.* The issue itself may be objective. Usually, both sides can agree on what issue is at stake. But differing viewpoints regarding the issue can be very subjective. For example, per-

haps one spouse wants to use his or her summer vacation to visit relatives, while the other spouse would prefer to take a cruise. The issue is clear, but the answer isn't. Both individuals can make good arguments for their preference. We should remember that, on most issues, God cares more about how we treat each other than He does about what decision we make. This helps us to see our disagreements in an entirely different light.

4. *In many disagreements, each side is valid.* No, this isn't some sort of postmodern, liberal rhetoric that denies absolute truth or an objective reality. Rather, this follows from the last point. Although we as individuals have limited perspectives regarding issues, this doesn't necessarily invalidate the perspectives that we do have. Each person is able to contribute something of value and worth to a discussion. And who knows? Perhaps the point of view we're ignoring or arguing against is just the key we need to help move us closer to the truth. Even a misguided contribution can highlight an important aspect of the truth!

When we disagree, it helps to keep in mind the various possibilities: (1) one of us may be right and the other, wrong; (2) both of us may be wrong; or (3) both of us may be partially right. Let's be honest. When we're in the midst of an argument, of course we think we're right—why else would we be arguing? However, we should enter into arguments with the expectation that any of the three possibilities above may be true. We may be completely wrong, and we may have to admit it. Or we may both be right, and, due to a misunderstanding or the complexity of the issue, our opinions complement each other rather than exactly coinciding. Or it may turn out that we're both wrong. We discover the truth through gracious discussion, not through contentious debate.

Think back on the last argument you had. Do you think you handled the argument with a gracious attitude? Why or why not?

_____

_____

_____

_____

A DISAGREEMENT BETWEEN TWO GODLY LEADERS

In the book of Acts, the four realities of disagreements we saw above take on human faces in the persons of Paul and Barnabas. The account of the argument between these Spirit-filled men demonstrates that disagreements are inevitable, even between godly people. Often, we must grapple to understand two or more subjective perspectives on an objective issue.

The Critical Issue

Acts 13 records a journey made by Paul and Barnabas, who had been set apart by the Holy Spirit to preach the gospel in Asia Minor. We call this Paul's first missionary journey (see Acts 13:1–3). John Mark, Barnabas's cousin, accompanied the two men as their assistant (13:4–5). He walked beside them during the first part of the trip, but as the trio sailed into Pamphylia, John Mark lost heart for some reason. Luke reports the simple truth: "John left them and returned to Jerusalem" (13:13). Barnabas and Paul continued on their journey, which no doubt became much more difficult without young John Mark's assistance. After experiencing success despite great hardships, the two ministers of the gospel returned to Antioch, their home base (Acts 13:14–14:28).

GETTING TO THE ROOT

In Acts, two different Greek words are used for John Mark's return to Jerusalem during the first missionary journey. In Acts 13:13, the author, Luke, used the more neutral term *apocho reo*, which means simply "to go away" or "leave."[1] However, in his argument against Barnabas, Paul used the phrase *aphiste mi*, which has a more negative connotation: to "desert."[2] In fact, from *aphiste mi* we get our word "apostatize," which means to defect or abandon one's faith.[3] While Barnabas probably had a neutral view of Mark's return to Jerusalem, Paul's view was definitely more negative.

Some time later, Paul proposed to Barnabas that they return to the places where they had traveled and preached in order to check on the welfare of the new believers (Acts 15:36). However, a critical issue arose between them on which they couldn't agree: "And

Barnabas was desirous of taking John, called Mark, along with them also" (15:37). To this suggestion, Paul replied in the absolute negative: "But Paul kept insisting that they should not take him along who had deserted them in Pamphylia and had not gone with them to the work" (v. 38). The issue was simple: should a person who leaves a mission be given a second chance? Paul said, "No, absolutely not." Barnabas said, "Yes, by all means."

THE OPPOSING VIEWPOINTS

The disagreement between Paul and Barnabas likely stemmed from their different personalities. Paul, more focused on the vital ministry of sharing the gospel, probably feared that taking Mark would result in another desertion. Barnabas, more focused on the young man's potential, believed Mark could grow into a great evangelist if only given the opportunity. Paul's passion for the mission clashed with Barnabas's compassion for the missionary. As a result, "a sharp disagreement" arose between them (Acts 15:39).

Paul and Barnabas verbally "duked it out." This was not a calm, logical argument, with the two men politely presenting positives and negatives and carefully weighing the issues. This was an outburst of strong words and heated emotions. One only hopes that John Mark wasn't present to hear it!

GETTING TO THE ROOT

The Greek word describing the disagreement between Paul and Barnabas is *paroxysmos*. It has come down to us in the English as the word *paroxysm*, which has essentially the same meaning: "a sudden violent emotion or action."[4] The word is also used in the Greek translation of the Old Testament to describe God's anger and wrath when He sent armies to judge Israel for their rebellion against Him (see Deuteronomy 29:27; Jeremiah 39:16).

Using Proverbs 25:19 and any other passages you can think of, try to argue for Paul's point of view for leaving Mark behind on the second trip.

_____

_____

_____

Using the account of Peter's restoration (John 13:37–38; 21:16) and any other passages you can think of, try to argue for Barnabas's point of view for bringing Mark along.

_____

_____

_____

_____

Put yourself in the place of Paul and Barnabas. How do you think you would have responded? Of the two men, who do you think was right? Were they both right, both wrong, or was only one right? Why?

_____

_____

_____

DIGGING DEEPER

The word *orthodoxy* might make some think of dogmatic, judgmental academics who hunt down heretics, rebuking anyone who disagrees with them on any detail. However, *orthodoxy*, which literally means "correct opinion," actually serves to unite Christians throughout the world rather than to divide them. This term refers to the central, essential doctrines of the Christian faith that distinguish it from all other religions and from cults.

J. I. Packer writes, "The term [*orthodoxy*] expresses the idea that certain statements accurately embody the revealed truth content of Christianity and are therefore in their own nature normative for the universal church. This idea is rooted in the NT insistence that the gospel has a specific factual and theological content (1 Corinthians 15:1–11; Galatians 1:6–9; 1 Timothy 6:3; 2 Timothy 4:3–4)."[5]

Obviously, not all issues debated by Christians are matters of orthodoxy. As believers, we should take the concept of orthodoxy to heart, spending more time focusing on our agreements concerning the central issues of the person and work of Christ, salvation by grace through faith, the Trinity, and the Bible, and less time arguing about matters that don't affect orthodoxy. If we do this, we might be able to avoid many sharp disagreements.

THE PERMANENT SEPARATION

How did these two faithful missionaries, fueled by a passion for the lost, resolve their disagreement? After their heated argument, Paul and Barnabas separated permanently. They never ministered together again. Acts 15:39–40 says, "They separated from one another, and Barnabas took Mark with him and sailed away to Cyprus. But Paul chose Silas and left."

Do you think it was God's plan for Barnabas and Paul to split up? Why or why not?

_____

_____

_____

_____

Years later, Paul spoke favorably of both Barnabas and Mark (see 1 Corinthians 9:6 and Colossians 4:10). What does this tell you about how disagreements among the godly should turn out?

_____

_____

_____

_____

Are there people against whom you are harboring a grudge due to a past disagreement? In light of Paul and Barnabas's story, what should you do?

_____

_____

_____

_____

MODELING GRACE THROUGH DISAGREEABLE TIMES

The Bible is filled with instructions for handling disagreements and disputes. Ephesians 4:29–32 addresses the proper attitude and heart from which we should approach any and every argument.

Read Ephesians 4:29–32. What are some examples of unwholesome, bitter, wrathful, and malicious words used in disagreements?

_____

_____

_____

_____

What are some examples of edifying, gracious, kind, and tender words used in disagreements?

_____

_____

_____

_____

Using Paul's principle of speaking edifying words that "give grace to those who hear" (Ephesians 4:29), let's consider four ways that we can handle our future disagreements with grace.

First, always leave room for an opposing viewpoint. Christian humility, wrought by the Spirit of grace, will help you to realize that you're not always right. And even when you *do* happen to be right, you can exercise love and patience toward those who have not yet been so "enlightened." Remembering the times when you've been proven wrong should help you to handle your disagreements with grace. Sometimes we just need to swallow our pride and keep our mouths shut!

Second, if an argument must occur, don't assassinate. An argument, even a strong argument, is one thing—it can be taken care of and brought to an end. But making it personal by verbally attacking the other person may leave lasting scars on that person's heart. Using words as weapons has nothing to do with edifying, and everything to do with destroying. Be civil!

Third, if you don't get your way, get over it and get on with life. If you feel you were right, but things didn't go your way in a relationship, a church, or a business, move past it. If you discover you were wrong and need to be corrected, show yourself and others some grace, and admit that you were wrong. Don't stew over the situation, endlessly replaying the events in your mind. Get over it!

Finally, sometimes the best solution is a separation. This shouldn't be your first option, but it may be necessary if you're dealing with serious issues. This decision should be made only after spending time in prayer and seeking God's wisdom for handling the situation.

Paul and Barnabas may have separated as a result of their anger, but if they had been able to discuss their perspectives reasonably they may still have decided that separation was the best solution. Perhaps God would have shown them the wisdom in separating, since that would help the two men to bear fruit over a greater area of Asia Minor. In addition, it would also give John Mark another chance to share in the ministry as Barnabas's partner.

When they must occur, separations from churches, ministries, or friends should be handled *graciously.* Even if you feel pain, loss, or anger, try to leave the relationship on good terms rather than just stomping out and slamming the door. Be gracious!

Do any of these four application points apply to a disagreement you're having now or have had in the past? Which ones? What can you do to apply these principles graciously?

_____

_____

_____

_____

To those who haven't thought through which issues in the Christian faith are worth *dying* for, it may seem that every minor doctrinal opinion is worth *fighting* for. If we're to stand firm on the primary, essential elements of the Christian faith and graciously allow for disagreements on "gray areas," we need to know what these gray areas are. C. S. Lewis once wrote, "When all is said (and truly said) about divisions of Christendom, there remains, by God's mercy, an enormous common ground."[6]

How would you assess the importance of the issues outlined on the next page?

Spreading Your Wings

ISSUE	WORTH DYING FOR	WORTH SEPARATING AND GOING A DIFFERENT ROUTE	WORTH GRACIOUSLY DEBATING/ DISCUSSING	LIFE IS TOO SHORT TO WORRY ABOUT
Is Jesus God?				
Correct method of baptism				
Is hell a place of literal fire?				
Style of worship				
Chairs or pews in the new sanctuary				
Are good works necessary for salvation?				
Choice of political party or candidate				
Are the gifts of the Holy Spirit for today?				
Is God a Trinity?				
Is drinking diet cola a sin?				
Priorities in mission work				
Coffee flavors in the church foyer				

Some things, such as those upon which people's eternal destinies depend, are worth dying for. Some things, such as matters concerning people's spiritual growth and spiritual health, are extremely important. Yet some things aren't worth spending even five minutes discussing. We need to discern the differences and be "diligent to preserve the unity of the Spirit in the bond of peace" (Ephesians 4:3). Jesus died and rose again to make us one in Him. God's kingdom doesn't advance when we fight over nonessentials, but when we graciously love one another. In the end, we want to care about what He cares about, and love as He loves.

In too many cases the battle goes on and on and on,
and the ministry becomes fractured because the opposing parties
are not big enough to get over the initial hurt. . . .
How many are living out their lives with their spiritual shades drawn,
thinking to themselves, "I'll have nothing more to do with the church,"
because of an argument they witnessed or maybe participated in?
We need to be people who can disagree in grace and then press on,
even if the disagreement leads to a separation.

—The Grace Awakening

10

GRACE: UP CLOSE AND PERSONAL

 Soaring on His Word

> *And we know that God causes all things to work together for good to those who love God, to those who are called according to His purpose. For those whom He foreknew, He also predestined to become conformed to the image of His Son, so that He would be the firstborn among many brethren.*
> —ROMANS 8:28–29

JOHN BUNYAN, a seventeenth-century tinker, had just begun serving his third jail term for preaching the gospel when he was led to write one of the most influential books in Christian history. Since then, Bunyan's imaginative allegory, *The Pilgrim's Progress*, has found its way into hearts and lives all around the world.

The Pilgrim's Progress takes the reader on a journey through life with a man named Christian. Along the way, Christian meets characters who personify the perils and struggles that believers face. With the aid of friends like Evangelist, Help, and Interpreter, Christian overcomes adversaries like Pliable, Obstinate, Hypocrisy, and Despair as he seeks to remove the heavy burdens of sin and guilt from his back. Christian faces few opponents more insidious than Worldly Wiseman and Mr. Legality, who threaten to undo Christian's new identity in Christ and restore his former name, Graceless. Christian's encounter with the threat of legalism is summed up well in the following verse:

> When Christians unto Carnal Men give ear,
> Out of their Way they go, and pay for't dear.

For Master Worldly Wiseman can but shew
A Saint the way to Bondage and to Wo.[1]

After his encounter with Mr. Legality, Christian comes to the home of Interpreter, who leads him to a large room full of dust (original sin). At first, someone attempts to clean the chamber with a broom (the law), but the broom merely kicks up the dust and makes the room unbearable. Only after someone else comes with water (grace) is the room completely cleansed. In *The Pilgrim's Progress*, it's clear that grace—not law—cleanses sin from a life.

Now that Christ has come into your life and removed the oppressive burdens of sin and guilt from your back, are you full of grace? Or do you still trudge along like a caterpillar instead of using your wings of grace? If you're using your wings, are they strong and stable, or weak and flimsy? Your answer to this depends on where you are in your own journey toward a grace awakening.

THE PATH THAT LEADS TO GRACE AWAKENING

There's a deadly, venomous serpent slithering around the heels of unsuspecting Christians as they seek to progress in their faith. It's the false doctrine of "sanctification through works"—the idea that we can grow in the Christian life as a result of our own limited human power.

By God's grace, when a person trusts in Christ alone for salvation, the Father declares the believer righteous—an act we call *justification*. Once a person has been justified by faith, God begins the day-by-day process of helping that believer reach spiritual maturity—a process called *sanctification*. Yet Christians sometimes forget that we are not only justified by grace through faith, but we're also sanctified by that same grace.

Ephesians 2:8–9 addresses our justification by grace through faith: "For by grace you have been saved through faith; and that not of yourselves, it is the gift of God; not as a result of works, so that no one may boast." However, we tend to forget about the next verse, which addresses our sanctification by God's sovereign plan and purpose: "For we are His workmanship, created in Christ Jesus for good works, which God prepared beforehand so that we would walk in them" (v. 10). God enables the process of our sanctification by His grace—not our works.

For each of the following passages on spiritual growth, write in the boxes who does the work, the results of it, and who benefits from it.

	WHO WORKS?	THE RESULTS?	WHO BENEFITS?
Romans 8:28–29			
Philippians 1:6			
Philippians 2:13			
Hebrews 13:20–21			

How does the knowledge that God's power is at work in your life affect your view of your spiritual growth?

_____

_____

_____

_____

As the process of sanctification unfolds according to God's grace in our lives, He uses certain tools to mold us toward Christlikeness. We can discern at least three ways in which God effects this process: time, pain, and change. Though these may seem to us more like weapons than tools at times, God is using them for His good purposes. Let's consider these for a moment.

 Time. Just as John Bunyan's character Christian needed time to travel from one place to the next on his arduous journey, it will also take time for God to work out His sovereign plan in our lives (see Hebrews 5:14).

 Pain. Just as Christian's progress involved weariness, perils, and woe, our own growth will involve painful events and circumstances (see Hebrews 12:4–13).

Change. Just as the pilgrim's journey resulted in a change of identity from Graceless to Christian, there is gracelessness in our lives that must be changed to graciousness (see Romans 12:1–2).

FLYING AGAINST THE WINDS OF OUR CULTURE

Take a moment to review our discussion of humanism in chapter 2. Webster defines *humanism* as "a doctrine, attitude, or way of life centered on human interests or values; especially a philosophy that usually rejects supernaturalism and stresses an individual's dignity and worth and capacity for self-realization through reason."[2]

How does the process of sanctification we've looked at in this chapter contrast with the humanist approach to spiritual growth?

_____

_____

_____

_____

CLAIMING GRACE

Many of us remember the classic children's story of Pinocchio. A loving toymaker named Geppetto created a wooden marionette whose greatest desire was to become a real boy. Though Pinocchio's quest involved lessons to learn and all sorts of obstacles that threatened to lead him on a path toward destruction, Pinocchio's dream ultimately came true. He was granted boyhood.

In some ways we as believers find ourselves in a similar process. We're somewhere on the path of being transformed from a hollow, wooden marionette to a grace-filled, living child of God.

Let's focus on five areas of our lives in which we all tend to struggle to grow in grace. There are areas in each of us that are still brittle wood—areas we resist releasing to God to be softened and molded into pliable authenticity. As we surrender these qualities to God and claim His transforming power, He will conform us more completely to the image of His Son.

REMOVING THE WOOD OF INSECURITY: CLAIMING THE GRACE TO BE WHAT WE ARE

In 1 Corinthians 15:8–9, Paul regarded himself as one "not fit to be called an apostle" and "the least of the apostles" because he had severely persecuted the church (see Acts 8:3). Having such a background would have caused many Christians to shy away from telling others about the kingdom of God. But, rather than focusing on his checkered past, Paul chose to concentrate on God's grace: "But by the grace of God I am what I am, and His grace toward me did not prove vain; but I labored even more than all of them, yet not I, but the grace of God with me" (1 Corinthians 15:10). Paul was honest with himself and his readers about who he

Thru many dangers, toils and snares,
I have already come;
'Tis grace hath brought me safe thus far,
And grace will lead me home.[3]

was and who he was becoming by God's grace. This freed him to embrace his new identity in Christ and to live it out with confidence (see Galatians 2:20).

What events or actions in your past make you insecure about your current role in the body of Christ? What steps can you take to overcome these obstacles?

_____

_____

_____

_____

REMOVING THE WOOD OF WEAKNESS:
CLAIMING THE GRACE TO LEARN FROM OUR SUFFERINGS

In 2 Corinthians 12:7–10, Paul informed his readers that God had allowed him to experience a serious physical ailment in order to keep him from exalting himself. When Paul requested that the Lord remove this affliction, God refused. Instead, He responded, "My grace is sufficient for you, for power is perfected in weakness" (12:9). In the weakness of Paul's suffering, God's glorious grace was most obvious to him, and it's the same for us.

In your service of Christ, what do you consider to be your greatest weaknesses?

_____

_____

_____

_____

In what ways has God used these weaknesses to teach you about Him? How has He demonstrated His grace to you in spite of these weaknesses?

_____

_____

_____

_____

REMOVING THE WOOD OF ABRASIVENESS:
CLAIMING THE GRACE TO RESPOND TO WHAT WE ENCOUNTER

Grace involves how we conduct ourselves with others, especially those who are not believers (see Colossians 4:5). Colossians 4:6 says, "Let your speech always be with grace, as though seasoned with salt, so that you will know how you should respond to each person."

Seasoning our speech with grace can be difficult, can't it? James 3:2–12 tells us, in no uncertain terms, that the tongue is *impossible* for people to tame by their own power. In fact, he described our tongues as "set on fire by hell" (3:6)! This means that abrasiveness is the norm, not the exception. Our tongues are set on "abrasive mode" by default, so we require God's divine reprogramming to change this expression of our natures.

Think of a recent situation in which you lost control of your tongue and spoke abrasively to a friend or family member. How could you have communicated your feelings in a way that was seasoned with grace rather than harshness?

_____

_____

_____

_____

REMOVING THE WOOD OF COMPROMISE: CLAIMING THE GRACE TO STAND FOR WHAT WE BELIEVE

The author of Hebrews exhorts us to be "strengthened by grace" rather than "carried away by varied and strange teachings" (Hebrews 13:9). We're called to imitate the faith of past believers—those who refused to back down from their convictions (see 13:7). The greatest example of spiritual stability and unwavering conviction, of course, was Jesus Christ. He is "the same yesterday and today and forever" (13:8).

In which areas of your life (at home, work, school, among friends, etc.) do you feel the greatest temptation to buckle under to pressure by compromising what you believe? Why?

If there is anything that will help strengthen the charming magnet of grace, it is the ability to laugh at oneself, to laugh at life, to find humor in everyday encounters with people. Talk about sprinkling salt to enhance the taste! Humor works like magic.

—*The Grace Awakening*

_____

_____

_____

_____

Read Ephesians 6:11–17. How can God's gracious provisions keep you standing without compromising in these areas?

_____

_____

_____

_____

REMOVING THE WOOD OF PRIDE:
CLAIMING THE GRACE TO SUBMIT TO WHAT I NEED

Drawing on passages such as Psalm 138:6; Proverbs 3:34; and Jesus's teaching in Matthew 23:12, James wrote, "But He gives a greater grace. Therefore it says, 'GOD IS OPPOSED TO THE PROUD, BUT GIVES GRACE TO THE HUMBLE'" (James 4:6). Similarly, Peter wrote, "You younger men, likewise, be subject to your elders; and all of you, clothe yourselves with humility toward one another, for GOD IS OPPOSED TO THE PROUD, BUT GIVES GRACE TO THE HUMBLE" (1 Peter 5:5). These passages encourage us to trust God for what we need in every circumstance, especially in the midst of trials and temptations. Because pride causes us to place confidence in our abilities rather than in God, it's the mortal enemy of humility.

What fortresses of pride in your life are causing you to forfeit the grace God gives to the humble (for example, your career, salary, home, accomplishments, etc.)?

_____

_____

_____

_____

Spreading Your Wings

Of the areas in your life that are still hardened, brittle wood, which require the most immediate attention? In the lists below, match your areas of need with the appropriate wood density.

_____ 1. Wood of Insecurity   a.   Pulp

_____ 2. Wood of Weakness   b.   Soft pine

_____ 3. Wood of Abrasiveness   c.   Cedar chips

_____ 4. Wood of Compromise   d.   Hard as oak

_____ 5. Wood of Pride   e.   Is this wood or metal?

Drawing on your responses, write a prayer below surrendering the top three areas of hardness to the softening of God's grace. Add this request for grace to your daily prayer list.

_____

_____

_____

_____

_____

_____

_____

_____

Grace is not only what transforms us, it's what enables us to admit our own struggles and to relate to others who may also be struggling with the wood of insecurity, suffering, abrasiveness, compromise, or pride. By not hiding or denying our weaknesses, we invite people in. Vulnerability helps others identify with and feel comfortable around us. When we find contentment even in our weaknesses, as Paul did (2 Corinthians 12:10), the anxiety that accompanies keeping up a good front vanishes, freeing us to be real.

If you have many areas in your life that are still hardened, hollow wood, don't despair! He who began a good work in you *will* bring it to completion (see Philippians 1:6).

CONTINUING THE JOURNEY

In our "pilgrim's progress" through life, some of us expect a walk in the park, not a search for the Holy Grail. While we encounter constant struggles against external challenges, we also face the personal trials that come with the difficult process of transformation.

Thankfully, our journey isn't over! God isn't finished with us yet. By His grace, He's still in the business of transforming our hearts of stone into hearts of flesh (see Ezekiel 11:19). One day, our journey as pilgrims will come to a glorious end as we reach heaven—the "Celestial City." Until then, we're called to press on with confidence and grace.

The real Son of God is at your side.

He is beginning to turn you into the same kind of thing as Himself.

He is beginning, so to speak, to "inject" His kind of life and thought . . .

into you; beginning to turn the tin soldier into a live man. The part of you

that does not like it is the part that is still tin. [4]

—C. S. LEWIS

11

ARE YOU REALLY A MINISTER OF GRACE?

 Soaring on His Word

You therefore, my son, be strong in the grace that is in Christ Jesus.

—2 TIMOTHY 2:1

MIKE ARRIVED ON THE NEW JOB SITE half an hour early. He was surprised to see several of the other laborers already at work—climbing ladders, cutting two-by-fours, and hauling materials back and forth. Mike flagged down a passing worker and asked where he could find Frank Smith. The worker mumbled and pointed to the construction site of a nearly completed two-story home, where a man lingered in the doorway, staring at his watch. Mike approached with his electrician's box in his left hand and his right extended for a handshake. "Good morning, Mr. Smith. I'm Mike Greenlee."

Frank Smith quickly dispensed with Mike's handshake and, pivoting on his heel like a soldier, ordered, "You're early, so you'll get started early. Follow me upstairs." As they ascended the winding stairway, Mike and Frank passed a young man installing molding along the base of the steps. Suddenly, Frank barked, "Hey, I thought I told you I wanted the flat molding!"

"This one was the same price. It matches the one in the hallway."

"You're not paid to think, Collins. Just follow the plans, and leave the thinking to me. I'll let it slide this time, but next time *ask first!*"

When Frank reached the second floor landing, he immediately started shouting at somebody down the hall. "Hey! I told you I wanted that Sheetrock finished by last night! I have a schedule to keep. You're slowing me down here!"

Frank led Mike into a large, unfinished room with a huge window. "We need to start the rewiring here. I fired the last electrician because he kept missing work—something about his kid in the hospital. Just as well, though. You seem like a hard worker."

As he set down his toolbox beneath the wide window, Mike caught sight of another building project next door. The house looked similar, though the project wasn't as far along as Frank's.

"That's Greg Moreno," Frank grumbled. "He started that house before I started this one, but just look at it. His guys are slow, they come and go as they please, and he's never around to keep an eye on them. His workers push him around. He'll never finish that house!"

From his bird's-eye view, Mike watched Greg passing out coffee and donuts to his workers. One laborer approached Greg with a copy of the building plans, grabbed a donut from the box, and asked Greg a question. The boss responded by shrugging his shoulders and signaling him to do the work the way he thought best. All of the workers looked happy, relaxed, and free. They were taking their time so they could do their very best work.

"Yep," Frank said, shaking his head in feigned pity, "Some of my lazy guys even went over to work for him. He sure doesn't know how to run a building project!" Frank strode from the room with a knowing smirk. Mike watched Greg continue to chat with his workers and motion to them with enthusiasm. Then Mike overheard Frank shouting at a plumber in the bathroom. A moment later, he began to argue with the drywall man again.

Mike made a decision. Grabbing his tools, he hurried down the stairs and out the front door. Instead of driving home, he cut across the lawn and onto the neighbor's property to introduce himself to Greg. After all, Greg might need a good electrician.

Consider for a moment this snapshot of two very different building projects. Frank Smith ran a tight ship; his style was characterized by negativity, selfishness, predictability, bossiness, and a lack of creativity—but he got things done! Greg, on the other hand, was generous and encouraging, allowing freedom of expression and creativity. For whom would you rather work?

Now, another question: When you're actually responsible for accomplishing something in work or ministry, are you more like Frank or Greg? In our task-oriented, accomplishment-driven society, many of us would prefer to be like Frank (and have Franks working for us) when we have to build a house or complete another important project. Yet ministry is as much about people as it is about purpose and projects, and the people of God are built up by grace.

Fictional Frank and imaginary Greg are not the only ones involved in building projects—we are, too. In 1 Corinthians 3:9–17,

WINDOWS TO THE ANCIENT WORLD

The construction of many ancient buildings began with the laying of a foundation of stone. A vital part of this foundation called the "cornerstone" helped align the entire building. When the superstructure was completed, the "capstone" was the final stone to be placed. Also known as the "top stone," this stone was placed at the top of a precipice, as the keystone in an arch, or in some other prominent location. Its placement indicated the official completion of a building project and—like the cornerstone, which marked the beginning—was cause for great celebration.[1]

Paul compared the church at Corinth to a building—in fact, a holy temple of the Spirit (3:16–17). The foundation of the Corinthian church was laid on the cornerstone of Jesus Christ. Paul warned, "According to the grace of God which was given to me, as a wise master builder I laid a foundation. . . . But each man must be careful how he builds on it" (3:10). Every believer within the local church was responsible for exercising his or her gifts as ministers to build up the body of Christ (3:11–15).

Did you catch that? You don't have to be a pastor or a worship leader to use your gifts for God's service. If you're in any way engaged deliberately and regularly in making Christ known, either to those in the body or those yet to be won to Christ, you're a minister! In light of Paul's words and the examples of Greg and Frank above, ask yourself: *Am I a minister of grace?*

What do you consider to be your primary ministry in your local church? If you don't currently have a ministry within the church, think about a past ministry experience or an area outside of church where you serve. Write it here.

_____

_____

_____

_____

Read 1 Corinthians 3:10. In your primary ministry, are you building "according to the grace of God"? Keeping in mind your primary ministry, answer the following questions as honestly and objectively as you can.

Do you give others the freedom to do things their own way?	❏ Yes	❏ No
Do people feel at ease rather than intimidated in your presence?	❏ Yes	❏ No
Do you encourage, build up, and affirm those to whom you minister?	❏ Yes	❏ No
Do you seek the glory of God rather than building your own ego?	❏ Yes	❏ No
Do you rely on God's Spirit of grace in ministry rather than your own power?	❏ Yes	❏ No
Do you seek the growth and welfare of those you minister with?	❏ Yes	❏ No
Do you see yourself as people driven rather than project driven?	❏ Yes	❏ No

A POWERFUL MESSAGE FROM A SPIRIT-DIRECTED PROPHET

Paul's description of the grace-oriented building project in 1 Corinthians 3 is not the only one of its kind in the Bible. In the book of Zechariah, we find the description of a physical building project that reveals an important contrast between reliance on divine grace and an attempt to use human power to accomplish God's work.

The temple of Solomon had been destroyed decades earlier, during the Babylonian invasion. Construction began on a new temple after Cyrus, the king of Persia, gave permission for Zerubbabel and several Jewish exiles to return to Jerusalem and restore their center of worship. When opposition arose, the inhabitants of the city gave up on the project and attended to their own comfortable lives. In response, God sent the prophets Haggai and Zechariah to urge the people to complete the task. While Haggai's rebuke was sharp, Zechariah's was gentle and creative. Prompted by these two prophets, the people of Jerusalem finally resumed their work on the temple.

TIMELINE OF EVENTS IN THE TEMPLE BUILDING PROJECT[2]	
586 BC	Nebuchadnezzar of Babylon destroyed Jerusalem and the temple.
538 BC	Cyrus of Persia issued a decree allowing Jews to return to their land and rebuild their temple.
536 BC	Work began on the temple under the leadership of Zerubbabel.
535 BC	Opposition to the building project from Samaritans and Arabs intensified.
534 BC	Temple construction ceased.
520 BC	At the urging of the prophets Haggai and Zechariah, work on the temple was resumed.
516 BC	Temple construction was completed.

In the midst of this project, as the workers were again becoming discouraged in the face of mountain-sized opposition from every side, an angel gave Zechariah a vision of a lampstand with seven lamps fed by the oil of two olive trees (Zechariah 4:1–3). Zechariah had no idea what this vision meant, so he asked the angel (4:4–5), who gave him the following answer:

> This is the word of the LORD to Zerubbabel saying, "Not by might nor by power, but by My Spirit," says the LORD of hosts. "What are you, O great mountain? Before Zerubbabel you will become a plain; and he will bring forth the top stone with shouts of 'Grace, grace to it!'" (Zechariah 4:6–7)

The oil represented the Holy Spirit, God's gracious source of power. The mountain represented the tremendous obstacles looming over Zerubabbel as he sought to complete the building. Through this vision, God was saying, "Zerubbabel, the obstacles before you that seem so insurmountable will be removed, and it won't be through your own might and power, but through My Spirit!"

Read Zechariah 4:7–10. If Zerubbabel had completed the building of the temple in his own power, write the words you think could have been written on the capstone (see the box, page 121) instead of "Grace, grace to it!"

_____

_____

_____

According to 1 Corinthians 10:31, what's ultimately wrong with ministry accomplished in our own strength?

_____

_____

GETTING TO THE ROOT

The two Hebrew words for "might" (chayil) and "power" (koach) used in Zechariah 4:6 ("not by might nor by power") often denote military might and manpower.[3] One commentator notes that the combination refers to "inherent power, courageous bravery, fortitude, as well as manpower, large numbers of soldiers, riches, leaders, well-coordinated organizations, good financial systems, etc."[4] God is saying it's not any of these things, but by His Spirit that the task will be accomplished.

The same warning about relying on human power rather than the power of the Holy Spirit applies to our building up the body of Christ, the New Testament temple of God (1 Corinthians 3:10–17). The problem is, human power gets results—often immediately—and it can be difficult to distinguish human work from that done by the power of the Spirit. The differences appear at the level of motives. Operating in the flesh reflects two main characteristics: (1) using human might to accomplish visible projects and (2) relying on personality power to manipulate people. What does it look like when we do it God's way? Let's focus on five obvious marks of a grace-awakening minister who relies on the Spirit rather than the flesh.

OBVIOUS MARKS OF A GRACE-AWAKENING MINISTER

Generosity with Personal Possessions (Absence of Selfishness)

Grace-oriented ministers are generous with their "personal" possessions. Instead of spouting the word *mine* all the time, they find ways in their areas of service to use the resources God has given them.

TWO CHARACTERISTICS OF OPERATING IN THE FLESH

Using human might in order to accomplish visible projects.

Relying on personality power to manipulate people.

Spreading Your Wings

Read Acts 4:32–35. What were the believers' attitudes toward material goods?

_____

_____

_____

_____

Make a list of the four personal possessions in your life that you hold most dear.

1.   My _____

2.   My _____

3.   My _____

4.   My _____

Now cross out the word *My* for each item and write in *God's*. How should this change your attitude toward these things?

_____

_____

_____

_____

Encouragement in Unusual Settings (Absence of Predictability)

Sometimes ministers find themselves in unusual and uncomfortable settings— among different kinds of people, in the midst of painful and awkward situations. Those who are ministering in the flesh have a tendency to flee from these new settings or to try to change their surroundings rather than adapt to the new situation. However, grace-oriented ministry frees itself from predictability and yields to the Spirit's direction as it seeks to engage the world in new contexts (see 1 Corinthians 9:19–23).

Read Acts 11:19–20. In verse 19, name the group to whom the Word was preached exclusively at first.

_____

_____

_____

_____

From verse 20, name the group to whom the disciples later preached the Word.

_____

_____

_____

_____

Read verses 21–23. When Barnabas came to encourage the ministry in Antioch, what did he witness, according to verse 23?

_____

_____

_____

_____

When Barnabas reached Antioch, he found a new setting. Rather than an all-Jewish congregation, there were Greeks everywhere! He saw the grace of God at work and he applauded it. He encouraged it. He adapted to it.

Life Beyond the Letter of the Scripture (Absence of Dogmatic Bible Thumping)

Handling God's work boldly and accurately is essential for those who minister. Care must be taken, however, to interpret and communicate it with grace. Paul told the Corinthians that the ministry of the new covenant is "not of the letter, but of the Spirit; because the letter kills, but the Spirit gives life" (2 Corinthians 3:6). Paul was contrasting old covenant law (found in the Bible of his day—the Old Testament) with the new covenant grace (the ministry of the Spirit). Paul still used the Old Testament Scripture as the source and center of his teaching, but he used it the right way—as a pointer to the grace of Christ. Peter, too, warned his readers that some teachers used the Bible—including New Testament writings—inappropriately (2 Peter 3:16–18).

Do you tend to view the Bible as a rule book to keep people in line, or as a road sign to point them to Christ by the power of the Spirit? How would you describe your experience with these two approaches in your own life and ministry?

_____

_____

_____

_____

Liberty for Creative Expression (Absence of Expectations)

In a grace-oriented ministry, there's a lack of rigid expectations, coupled with the freedom to allow creative expression. Paul tells us in 2 Corinthians 3:17, "Where the Spirit of the Lord is, there is liberty." Allowing freedom of expression among those to whom we minister is difficult because it seems so risky! What if you don't like the way they perform a task? What if you can do it better and faster? Yet grace-oriented ministry encourages others to use their gifts with freedom—even when that means making mistakes.

In your area of ministry, do you encourage individuality and freedom, or do you set a rigid standard others must follow?

_____

_____

_____

How can you encourage creative expression in your life, home, work, and ministry?

_____

_____

_____

_____

FLYING AGAINST THE WINDS OF OUR CULTURE

During the "reality TV" craze of recent years, a prime-time series called *The Apprentice* quickly shot to the top. The premise was simple. A group of contestants with various educational backgrounds, leadership styles, and business experiences was selected to compete for an executive internship in one of billionaire Donald Trump's companies. Following the mantra "It's just business, nothing personal," *The Apprentice* vividly illustrated the bankruptcy of graceless endeavors.

In their business ventures, many of the participants exhibited selfish, childish, rigid, and shameful behavior. The strongest personalities dominated, while the ideas of the timid or disliked participants were shot down. The contestants followed the rules when it suited them, but threw ethics out the window when their situations became desperate. Worst of all, leaders were willing to turn on their closest team members to avoid hearing Donald Trump's now-famous phrase, "You're fired!"

As we compare our own ministry experiences with the often graceless ventures of the business world, sometimes they turn out to be shamefully similar. While businesses rarely run like grace-oriented ministries, ministries often run like graceless businesses.

Release from Past Failures (Absence of Shame)

A minister of grace doesn't keep bringing up a person's past failures—and there will be some of these in any ministry. In 1 Timothy 1:12–13, Paul said that even though he had once been a blasphemer of Christ and persecutor of the church, he learned that God's grace for ministry was "exceedingly abundant." It covered Paul's past failures and freed him from the shame and guilt that holds many of us back.

Trace Paul's attitude toward John Mark's usefulness in ministry by reading Acts 15:37–39; Colossians 4:10; and 2 Timothy 4:11. Which people in your life might you be holding back because of their past failures or present inadequacies?

_____

_____

_____

_____

Many people attempt to build their ministries with might and power rather than by the Spirit. Instead of "Grace, grace to it!" many churches would rather inscribe on their capstones, "We did it! We did it!" Frankly, those ministries won't last. And, as long as they do, they'll hurt people and ultimately dishonor the Lord of grace. Though goals may not be accomplished instantly, ministry built by the power of the Spirit is characterized by grace. It's absent of selfishness, predictability, dogmatism, rigid expectations, manipulation, guilt, and shame. It lets people go, allowing God to use them according to His plan and purpose, not our own.

Now, ask yourself again: Am I *really* a minister of grace?

Stand up, stand up for Jesus,
Stand in His strength alone;
The arm of flesh will fail you—
Ye dare not trust your own;
Put on the gospel armor,
Each piece put on with prayer;
Where duty calls, or danger,
Be never wanting there. [5]

—GEORGE DUFFIELD, JR.

12

A MARRIAGE OILED BY GRACE

 Soaring on His Word

Nevertheless, each individual among you also is to love his own wife even as himself, and the wife must see to it that she respects her husband.

— EPHESIANS 5:33

*F*EW SOUNDS ARE MORE UNPLEASANT than the grinding of gears or the squeaking of hinges. When the gears in our cars slip, we rush to a mechanic. When our front doors creak, we use a lubricant on the hinges. When our joints make popping sounds, we run to the doctor. Yet when the gears of our marriage grind, many of us accept the noise as unavoidable. We tend to ignore friction in our marriages that we would never tolerate in our other relationships.

Some of us treat our spouses with respect in public but do the opposite in private. When our doors are shut, our blinds are pulled down, and our neighbors and friends can't see, the true husband and wife emerge from behind our pleasant social façades. Because the unseen gears of our marriages make close and constant contact, the oil of grace needs to flow abundantly between them.

Although this chapter focuses on marriage, its principles may be applied to any interpersonal relationship. If you are single, we encourage you to read the material and answer the questions in light of other close relationships. If you can exhibit grace in a relationship that brings you into close contact with the same person day after day, you can demonstrate grace to the people you see less regularly. If grace flows in the most difficult case, it should flow in the least difficult too.

FLYING AGAINST TYHE WINDS OF OUR CULTURE

In a media-driven culture like ours, where glamour is valued more than goodness, where fame is coveted above faithfulness, and where charisma means more than character, we encounter many people who are polished and presentable on the outside but are just plain rotten on the inside. Eugene Peterson gives us some insight into this contradiction:

> Is it possible to exhibit grace in your conduct in the kitchen as well as in a nationally televised debate?
>
> I once knew a man well who had a commanding public presence and exuded charm to all he met. What he said *mattered*. He had *influence*. He was always impeccably dressed and unfailingly courteous. But his secretary was frequently in tears as a result of his rudely imperious demands. Behind the scenes he was tyrannical and insensitive. His public image was flawless; his personal relationships were shabby.[1]

What's lacking in people like the man mentioned above? The same thing that's lacking in much of our culture: the refreshing, enabling oil of grace.

How do we inject the oil of grace into our marriages? How do we determine where our gears are grinding the loudest? So that we may experience a grace awakening in our marriages, let's turn to the Scriptures to find the answers to these questions.

Three major New Testament passages go into great detail to describe the points of friction in marriage and to prescribe the application of grace. These passages outline the three Rs of marriage: *realities*, *responsibilities*, and *roles*. Let's examine each of these in order.

THE GRACE TO FACE MARITAL REALITIES

Reality is a popular buzzword today. News features are called "reality checks," computers use "virtual reality" technology, and the naïve are said to require a "dose of reality." At the same time, many marital realities are often overlooked or misunderstood. First Corinthians 7 addresses at least three of these realities that many married couples would rather avoid. These realities often clash violently with the "alternate realities" fed to us by the grace-killing world in which we live.

First reality: Marriage requires mutual unselfishness. In 1 Corinthians 7:3–5, Paul wrote specifically about mutual obligations regarding sexual intimacy, but the application is much broader. The key element here is *unselfishness.* In marriage, the husband and wife no longer have authority over their own persons; rather, they have obligations to fulfill toward each other.

Read 1 Corinthians 7:3–5. In which areas of your marriage relationship does your selfishness most often appear? How does this selfishness cause friction?

_____

_____

_____

_____

Second reality: Marriage means a lifelong commitment. Paul's argument in 1 Corinthians 7:10–11 can be summed up in this statement: "When you marry, you marry for life." The world often rejects or forgets the reality of marital commitment. In our culture of no-fault divorce, the grounds for separation often contrast sharply with the commands of Scripture. In fact, the Bible *never* promotes divorce. God allows for divorce only in certain rare circumstances, and even then, He permits it only because of the hardness of people's hearts.

Today, people divorce on the legal grounds of discord or conflict of personalities, irreconcilable differences, irretrievable breakdown of the marriage relationship, or even incompatibility of temperament. While communication problems and personality conflicts may exist in most marriages, the root problem lies in the level of commitment rather than in the quality of the relationship. Scripture reminds us that we need a high level of commitment to make our marriages work. And, in the face of very real discord, this commitment only comes through God's grace.

Years ago Cynthia and I took the ugly word divorce *out of our dialogues. We agreed that we would not even store it in the arsenal of our argument vocabulary. No matter how heated our disagreements may be, we'd not threaten each other with that term. It does something to a marriage when you can count on your partner to stick around and hammer out your differences with each other instead of walking away from them.*

—The Grace Awakening

Read 1 Corinthians 7:10–13. Considering the number of times Paul instructs his readers not to "send away" their husbands or wives, what do you think this implies about the seriousness of the marriage commitment?

_____
_____
_____
_____

Third reality: Marriage includes times of trouble. The call to marital commitment implies that we'll have tough times. Paul specifically developed this truth in 1 Corinthians 7:26–28. Paul warned his un-married readers not to enter into marriage hastily because, as all of us who are married know, marriage brings "trouble in this life" (v. 28). The Bible doesn't sugarcoat the reality that married life offers its share of sorrows as well as joys.

From the following list, which do you consider to be the two most troubling points of friction in your marriage?

❑ Communication
❑ Finances
❑ Unmet Needs
❑ Intimacy
❑ Priorities
❑ Other

Assuming that you and your spouse may continue to disagree on these topics, describe how you could apply the oil of grace to ease the friction.

Scripture calls us to adopt attitudes and actions characterized by grace so that we can accept and live with the realities of marriage. Without the application of grace, the gears of our relationships will grind and eventually bring our marriages to a screeching halt. Don't let this happen to you! Make the choice to apply grace now.

THE GRACE TO ACCEPT PERSONAL RESPONSIBILITIES

As we grow from infancy to maturity, we learn to accept increasing levels of responsibility, whether we like it or not. Ephesians 5 presents Christians with responsibilities unique to husbands and wives. Neglecting these responsibilities brings discord and conflict, but fulfilling them doesn't come easily. It requires divine wisdom and power given to us by God's grace.

Paul urged his readers to be careful how they walked, not as unwise but as wise, understanding what the will of God is (Ephesians 5:15–17). According to James 1:5, how can believers achieve such wisdom?

According to Ephesians 5:18–21, what are the practical results of being filled with the Spirit? How might exhibiting these change the climate of your marriage, friendships, or other family relationships?

Some have taught the subjects of husband-wife responsibilities to such a severe extreme that little room is left to breathe on one's own or to think things through. On the other hand, these (and related verses) have been twisted and altered so much that their original impact has sometimes been neutralized. I want to guard against both extremes.

—The Grace Awakening

The wise fulfillment of our responsibilities according to God's will is not something that comes from our own strength but from the Holy Spirit by God's grace. The oil of grace will not flow in our horizontal relationships with others unless we first receive empowering grace from God in our vertical relationship with Him.

The wife's primary responsibility—to know herself so well and to respect herself so much that she gives herself to her husband without hesitation (Ephesians 5:22–24). It takes a heaping portion of grace to fulfill this marital responsibility and to release control. It takes grace from God for a wife to accept it and grace toward her husband for her to live it.

Read Ephesians 5:22–24. Which aspects of the responsibility of the wife do you think are the most difficult for you to accept and practice? Why?

_____

_____

_____

_____

The husband's primary responsibility—to love his Lord so deeply and to like himself so completely that he gives himself to his wife without conditions. While God expects the wife to respect her husband so much that she lives for him, He exhorts her husband to love his wife so much that he would die for her. Ephesians 5:25 says, "Husbands, love your wives, just as Christ also loved the church and gave Himself up for her."

Read Ephesians 5:25–30. Which aspects of the husband's responsibility do you think are the most difficult for you to accept and practice? Why?

The kind of unconditional love that characterizes the responsibilities of husbands and wives doesn't flow from our naturally fallen natures but requires the oil of grace. Without grace, human love becomes demanding, conditional, and self-seeking.

The better acquainted we become with the grace of God, the less threatened we feel by our responsibility to submit to authority. We also become less eager to abuse our own authority over others. Grace oils the gears of authority and submission so they work together and turn easily, rather than grinding noisily against each other. Ephesians 5:33 describes how these wheels of marriage operate when well oiled by grace: "Nevertheless, each individual among you also is to love his own wife even as himself, and the wife must see to it that she respects her husband."

DIGGING DEEPER

The principle of headship and submission is not an arbitrary structure that changes with the times but an established order consistent with God's own relationship with the world. The relationship between God the Father and His Son, Jesus Christ, also demonstrates this beautiful dynamic. The Father, Son, and Holy Spirit are eternal and equal in their power and deity (John 1:1; 5:18; 17:5). However, each has a specific role in His work in creation.

The gospels tell us that the Son voluntarily subjects His will to the Father's (Luke 22:42; John 5:30; 17:11). Paul taught that this ordered relationship between the Father and the Son should be mirrored in an ordered relationship between husbands and wives (1 Corinthians 11:3). Men and women are equal in their human nature and value; however, the wife should voluntarily accept her husband's headship, and the husband should voluntarily love his wife and take the role of godly leadership in his family.

When it comes to our responsibilities in marriage, it's easy for husbands and wives to lean toward one extreme or another. A husband may become a pushover who fails to provide physical and spiritual leadership in the home while his wife runs over him like a steamroller. On the other hand, a wife who has little self-respect may cater to every demand of a domineering husband and fail to provide the wise, loving accountability he needs to thrive in his leadership responsibilities.

In other instances, the husband and wife may battle over leadership in the home on a daily basis. Or, to the other extreme, both may be so timid and indecisive that their family responsibilities are neglected. But grace in marriage releases and affirms; it doesn't smother. Grace in marriage values the dignity of individuals; it doesn't destroy. Grace supports and encourages; it isn't jealous or suspicious.

Which of the following do you feel most accurately describes your marriage relationship?

❏ dominant husband—dominant wife ⟶ constant conflict

❏ timid husband—timid wife ⟶ lack of leadership

❏ dominant husband—timid wife ⟶ neglect of responsibilities

❏ timid husband—dominant wife ⟶ conflict and confusion of responsibility

❏ loving husband—respectful wife ⟶ proper balance of leadership and submission

With regard to your marriage role, where does the oil of grace need to be applied in your marriage to bring it closer to the ideal balance described in Ephesians 5:18–33?

_____

_____

_____

_____

THE GRACE TO FULFILL DISTINCT ROLES

The subject of gender roles has become a hot topic in today's culture due to the blurring of distinctions between male and female, masculine and feminine. In an age when terms like *heterosexual, homosexual,* and *metrosexual* flood the media, the traditional roles of husbands and wives described in 1 Peter 3 may appear obsolete and even ridiculous to some. Yet Christian couples, as joint heirs of the grace of life, have been called to embrace particular biblical responsibilities, regardless of the popularity of these roles in the eyes of the world (see 1 Peter 3:7).

The wife's role is to model true femininity through character traits that are precious to God and impressive to her husband. This includes not only her responsibility of submission (1 Peter 3:1–2) but also an emphasis on her inner character over her outer appearance (3:3–4). Needless to say, every wife needs God's grace to fulfill her role in marriage, especially if she has an unbelieving or disobedient husband.

Read 1 Peter 3:1–2. How should a wife respond to her husband's leadership, even if he isn't a believer or is disobedient to Christ? According to Peter, why should she respond this way?

_____

_____

_____

Read 1 Peter 3:3–4. In your marriage, do you tend to place more value on the inner character qualities that are displayed inside the home, or on the superficial, outer beauty that others see?

_____

_____

_____

_____

 GETTING TO THE ROOT

In 1 Peter 3:2, Peter says that a disobedient husband will "observe" his wife's good works and be won "without a word" (1 Peter 3:1). The Greek word for observe (*epopteuō*) implies grasping something "over a longer period of time through thoughtful observation."[2] This suggests that the wife's chaste and respectful behavior should not be "hit or miss" but consistently present.

Spreading Your Wings

In his book *His Needs, Her Needs,* Dr. Willard Harley lists five major "felt needs" of men and women, which he compiled from more than twenty years of marriage counseling. His findings are listed below.[3]

FIVE MAJOR NEEDS OF WOMEN	FIVE MAJOR NEEDS OF MEN
1. Affection	1. Sexual fulfillment
2. Conversation	2. Recreational companionship
3. Honesty and openness	3. An attractive spouse
4. Financial support	4. Domestic support
5. Family commitment	5. Admiration

Read 2 Corinthians 9:8; 12:9; and Hebrews 4:16, which assert that God's grace will provide for all your needs. By the all-sufficient grace of God, in what ways can you attempt to meet your spouse's needs in each of the areas listed above?

1. _____
2. _____
3. _____
4. _____
5. _____

In what specific ways can you work at applying the oil of grace to your spouse's efforts to meet your needs in each area?

1. _____
2. _____
3. _____
4. _____
5. _____

The husband's role is to model genuine masculinity, unselfishness, and sensitive leadership that strengthens the home and gives dignity to his wife. First Peter 3:7 instructs each husband to "show [his wife] honor as a fellow heir of the grace of life."

Several important observations can be made here about the nature of the husband-wife relationship. "Fellow" implies *mutual equality* before God. "Heir" implies *mutual dignity* in spiritual position. "Grace" implies *mutual humility* toward God and each other. And "life" implies *mutual destiny*. A home characterized by these four qualities will be a magnet of grace—not only for the parents and children, but also for families observing from the outside.

No one can have real happiness in marriage
who does not recognize in firm faith
that this estate together with all its works,
however insignificant,
is pleasing to God and
precious in His sight. [4]

— MARTIN LUTHER

13

THE CHARMING JOY OF GRACE GIVING

 Soaring on His Word

Each one must do just as he has purposed in his heart, not grudgingly or under compulsion, for God loves a cheerful giver. And God is able to make all grace abound to you, so that always having all sufficiency in everything, you may have an abundance for every good deed.
— 2 CORINTHIANS 9:7–8

IN CHARLES DICKENS'S *A Christmas Carol*, a mysterious power transformed Ebenezer Scrooge from a miserable miser into a generous giver. And, although it's not accompanied by the ghosts of Christmases past, present, and future, this power does possess a strangely magical quality.

What is this incredible power? It's the *joy of giving*. It may be found in the excitement of a husband as he watches his wife open the anniversary gift he bought her. It appears in the wide eyes of a three-year-old as he gives his daddy a hand-colored picture of his family. It's reflected in the satisfaction a volunteer feels after tutoring and mentoring a child. The joy of giving is a powerful, concrete experience of grace. The joy we feel when we give reflects God's own "grace giving"—grace that gives with no thought of receiving anything in return.

Think of a time when you experienced great joy and delight in giving to another. What were the circumstances? What was the gift?

Even though we often enjoy giving, most of us hate to be *told* to give. Have you ever beamed with delight when you mailed out your income or property tax payment? Not likely. Unless we're members of the church's deacon board or budget committee, most of us would rather not sit through a sermon on giving. In fact, you may have been tempted to skip this chapter entirely once you discovered that it focuses on giving! Many of us get uncomfortable and defensive when we have to address our attitude toward—and practice of—biblical giving.

WHAT MAKES US SO DEFENSIVE?

Why do we tend to get defensive when someone brings up the topic of giving? Here are three main reasons.

First, requests for giving can seem terribly repetitive. When we hear nothing but requests for money coming at us from all sides, we begin to block out those requests. Everywhere we turn, we find someone asking for money—on TV, on the radio, via mail and e-mail, at our front doors, in sermons, and even at the homes of friends and relatives.

Second, giving has become commercialized. When Christmas rolls around, we sometimes forget about the priceless gift that came freely to us so long ago—a Baby wrapped in swaddling clothes and lying in a manger. Instead, as consumers, we're pressured to buy, buy, buy! This profit-oriented, commercialized mentality is even found in our churches. Church members are pressured to give until it hurts, and then give some more. Fund-raising methods, too, often appear commercialized. Sometimes we wonder whether the purpose of a particular ministry or church truly is to serve God and people or simply to raise money.

Third, we get defensive because *some people have a hidden agenda.* Preachers sometimes harp on their congregation's obligation to give specific percentages or dollar amounts, using guilt tactics and manipulative methods. The bottom line to such messages is, not surprisingly, the bottom line—how much money can be made.

Think of a time when someone used guilt or pressure to try to compel you to give. What emotions and attitudes did you have about this experience?

_____

_____

_____

Let's now contrast the negative approaches to giving, which put us on the defensive, with Paul's grace-oriented approach in 2 Corinthians. Here we find principles that lead to joyful—even addictive—grace giving.

What Makes Giving So Wonderfully Addictive?

Depression plagued the "mother church" in Judea. No, the Judean believers weren't spiritually distraught, emotionally distressed, or morally derailed; they were financially bankrupt. For several years, Paul and other apostles had come to the aid of the poor in the Jerusalem church (Romans 15:25–27; Galatians 2:10). As did the churches in the region of Galatia and Macedonia, the church in Corinth had agreed to contribute to the support of the Jerusalem church (1 Corinthians 16:1–3). However, since the time Paul had written the letter of 1 Corinthians, the church had not yet fulfilled its commitment to giving (2 Corinthians 8:6). So the apostle wrote 2 Corinthians 8–9 to provide instructions for making a joyous commitment to giving.

Various circumstances and attitudes can prevent us from giving more to the Lord's work. List three common reasons why people hold back from giving.

1. _____
2. _____
3. _____

Read 2 Corinthians 8:1–5. According to the example of the Macedonians' giving, do you think any of the three reasons you listed above are legitimate? Why or why not?

How and why we give is of far greater significance to God than what we give. Attitude and motive are always more important than amount. Furthermore, once a person cultivates a taste for grace in giving, the amount becomes virtually immaterial. When those age-old grace killers, guilt and manipulation, are not used as leverage, the heart responds in generosity. Giving at that point becomes wonderfully addictive.

—The Grace Awakening

_____

_____

_____

_____

From Paul's description of the Macedonians' giving in 2 Corinthians 8:1–5, we learn that these believers actually *begged* the apostle to allow them to give, even though they suffered financial hardships themselves. The Macedonians' commitment to such financial liberality began with their commitment to the Lord and to the work of the apostles. Their money and resources naturally followed the leading of their hearts.

What was it that made giving so addictive for the Macedonians? We can identify at least four reasons.

First, joyous giving helps us keep a healthy balance. The church in Corinth was an extremely gifted one (1 Corinthians 1:4–7) that abounded "in everything" (2 Corinthians 8:7). While a church may possess great teaching, inspirational fellowship, gifted leaders, and committed followers, that church can only achieve balance when it gives itself to the Lord and His work, expressed through the giving of its resources. As Christians, we need to be balanced in the intake and output of our gifts.

Read 2 Corinthians 8:7. What was the purpose of God's blessings to the Corinthians?

_____

_____

_____

_____

In what ways has God blessed you? How would you compare the input and output levels of giving in your own life?

_____

_____

_____

Second, when we give, we model the same grace of Jesus Christ. Compelled by love and grace, the eternal Son of God willingly left the riches of His heavenly home and became the God-Man, Jesus, to take on the sins of the world and die in our place. He did so by grace, not compulsion. No band of angels forced the Son of God to "walk the plank" of heaven. God the Father didn't have to manipulate Him into becoming a man. Christ's amazing love and infinite grace led Him to give all He had for us (2 Corinthians 6:9).

Third, when we give, we counteract selfishness and covetousness. Although the church at Corinth had zealously committed to give to the work of the apostles, the people apparently had failed to follow through on their commitment. Without assuming the reason for this, Paul wanted to make sure it was not from selfish motives (2 Corinthians 9:1–5).

Fourth, you can't help but be generous when grace consumes you. Second Corinthians 9:6 makes this bold warning and promise: "Now this I say, he who sows sparingly will also reap sparingly, and he who sows bountifully will also reap bountifully."

This principle represents neither magic nor a formula for making a profit. We find a similar principle in Malachi 3:10, where God made a bold promise to the Israelites who were faithful in their temple tithe: "Bring the whole tithe into the storehouse, so that there may be food in My house, and test Me now in this," says the Lord of hosts, "if I will not open for you the windows of heaven and pour out for you a blessing until it overflows."

The secret is not making more money. No one ever changed his or her giving pattern strictly because of increased income. I repeat, the focus should not be on the amount of money someone makes. Our Lord rarely emphasized that. Rather, His concern is on what one gives and the importance of releasing it in grace. What a wonderful way to counteract selfishness and covetousness. You will find that when grace awakens within you, selfishness will no longer win the day!

—The Grace Awakening

Have you ever hesitated to give for fear of "breaking the bank"? How does 2 Corinthians 9:6 address this concern?

_____

_____

_____

_____

WHAT MAKES GRACE GIVING SO ATTRACTIVE?

We've seen why the topic of giving makes us so defensive. We've also discovered why giving can be wonderfully addictive. Now, let's examine four reasons why we find grace giving so attractive.

The first reason we appreciate grace giving is that *grace individualizes the gift.* Paul wrote in 2 Corinthians 9:7, "Each one must do just as he has purposed in his heart." God not only wants us to give out of overflowing grace, but He wants our gifts to be unique. Interestingly, Paul never told his readers how much or what percentage of their income they were to give. He didn't even mention the word *money.* Instead, he left both the amount and the kind of gift to the individual.

If all Christians were reduced to a welfare income and they tithed on that a-mount, the church would double its receipts.[1]

—Ronald Blue

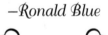

Giving involves planning and purpose. When it's time to give, we as believers shouldn't just pull out whatever spare change we may have in our pockets at the moment. Instead, we should work regular giving into our budget and, if married, establish a giving plan with our spouse.

The second reason we find grace giving so attractive is that *grace makes the action joyfully spontaneous.* The second part of 2 Corinthians 9:7 says that we are to give "not grudgingly or under compulsion; for God loves a cheerful giver." Often, we treat the passing of the offering plate at church more like a funeral than a celebration.

Some people even look like they'd rather be taking money out than putting it in! However, Paul reminds us that grace giving should be a joyful experience.

If you view giving to the Lord's work as a joyless burden, why *do* you give? Examine your motives. Do you tend to give out of obligation, peer pressure, seeking God's favor, or for some other reason?

_____

_____

_____

_____

_____

If you struggle with joyless giving, talk over the issue with God. Ask Him to help you to have a heart like His when it comes to giving, and ask how He would want you to respond to this issue.

The third reason we find grace giving so attractive is that *grace enables us to link up with God's supply line.*

GETTING TO THE ROOT

The Greek word translated "cheerful" in 2 Corinthians 9:7 is *hilaros.* Though we derive from it the English word *hilarious,* the original Greek meaning is far deeper than a boisterous laughter as the English may sometimes indicate.[2] *Hilaros* implies gladness, merriment, or joyfulness[3]—a deep attitude of the heart rather than merely a superficial giddiness. Paul indicates that not only are we as believers to give willingly, but we're to give with a joyful attitude that neither hesitates nor regrets. Eugene Peterson renders the verse this way in *The Message:* "God loves it when the giver delights in the giving."

If you've ever watched floodwaters rush from their source and flow across dry land, you know that the water always takes the path of least resistance. In a similar way, God sends more resources through those who graciously serve as fast-flowing conduits of grace. Increased giving not only benefits the giver, but it equips that person with an abundance of resources so he or she can continue to bless others. We don't give just so God will bless us; on the contrary, God blesses us so we can give more abundantly.

Read Proverbs 11:25; Luke 6:38; and Philippians 4:19. What promise does God give to those who are generous with what He has given them?

_____

_____

_____

_____

The fourth reason we find grace giving so attractive is that *grace leads to incomparable results.* Second Corinthians 9:13–14 reveals at least three incomparable results of grace giving:

1. Others give God the glory.

2. Others learn, by example, to be generous.

3. The relationship between giver and receiver can be deepened.

Sometimes, we see immediate results from our giving. At other times, we must wait to see the fruit of our gifts. In our fast-food and microwave culture, we like to reap immediately the rewards of our labor. But we need to get over this instant-gratification mentality! We're called to give confidently, trusting that God will work through our contributions whether we see the results or not.

Spreading Your Wings

If God were to examine your checkbook register or bank statement, what would He find? How do your monetary gifts to the Lord's work compare to the money you spend on entertainment, recreation, and luxuries?

_____
_____
_____
_____

God invites us to become cheerful givers with Him. What greater blessings might you receive by giving to His work rather than spending your money on your own desires most of the time?

_____
_____
_____
_____

Read Acts 4:33–35. How did the earliest believers express the "abundant grace" that God lavished upon them? How can you express this same abundant grace?

_____
_____
_____
_____

Read Luke 14:13–14 and 1 Timothy 6:18–19. What reward is promised to those who are generous with what God has given them? Does this motivate you to give more of your resources? Why or why not?

_____
_____
_____
_____

Paul, the apostle of grace, concluded his discussion of giving with this exclamation: "Thanks be to God for His indescribable gift!" (2 Corinthians 9:15). When Paul wanted to describe God's ultimate act of grace giving—the gift of His only begotten Son (John 3:16)—he had no words to do so. The gift truly was indescribable. Indeed, when it comes to our own grace giving, God's act is tough for us to follow! We need a grace awakening. Only by means of an overflow of grace—not by compulsion or guilt—can our own giving even begin to approach that of God when He offered us this "indescribable gift."

Biblical grace, by definition,
is a gift so immense,
it is unrepayable.
When you give or receive a grace gift,
you are suddenly in the presence of
something too immense to be repaid.[4]

—CALVIN MILLER

14
GRACE: IT'S REALLY ACCEPTING!

 Soaring on His Word

A man can receive nothing unless it has been given him from heaven.

—JOHN 3:27

AGAINST THE BACKDROP OF THE POLITICAL UPHEAVAL in nineteenth-century France, Victor Hugo's novel *Les Miserables* paints a stark contrast between two men's responses to grace. After spending nineteen years in prison for stealing a loaf of bread, the hero, Jean Valjean, assaults and robs a priest who had given him a place to stay on his first night out of prison. Valjean then disappears into the night, but the police quickly catch him with the silver dishes and utensils he has stolen. They march him back to the priest's home. With Valjean's destiny in his hands, the priest makes a choice. He tells the police that he gave Valjean the silver as a gift and even offers Valjean his wife's prized silver candlesticks. The priest's act of pure grace permanently changes Valjean, and he spends the rest of his life extending grace and kindness to others.

In contrast to the priest, Valjean's nemesis—the vindictive police inspector Javert—values strict justice above all else. Convinced that no criminal can ever change, Javert relentlessly pursues Valjean for years for violating his parole. In an unusual turn of events, a band of young people caught up in a rebellion against the French government eventually captures Javert and turns him over to Valjean for the people's justice. Rather than killing Javert, however, Valjean extends grace to his enemy, sparing the policeman's life. This act of mercy finally convinces Javert that the ex-con has, in fact, changed, and that Valjean's way of grace is superior. Yet, rather than abandoning his hunt for Valjean, which would contradict his duty under the law, Javert realizes that he'll never be able to stop chasing him. As a result, the policeman casts himself into a river and drowns. This conflicted, miserable man's refusal to let go of the law and accept grace ultimately leads to his death.

Grace that is truly amazing is truly *accepted*. If we, like Javert, refuse to accept grace, we will never know its freedom. While God offers His grace to everyone, only some see their need for it, humble themselves, and receive it. Some people respond to God's grace like a parched desert traveler finding a refreshing watering hole—he cups his hands to bring the cool refreshment to his lips once, then again, and again until his thirst is quenched. These people recognize their need for grace and race to receive God's supply. Others turn away from God's offer of grace because they think they can live life on their own. This is even true of many Christians who have accepted God's grace for salvation but embrace self-sufficiency in their daily lives.

The truth is that having an independent attitude toward God blocks us from both receiving God's grace and extending it to others. When we assert our self-sufficiency, trying to rely on our own strengths and abilities, we're like a freshly waxed car that won't start because of a corroded battery. Though our outsides may be polished, our hardened hearts block the flow of grace.

ROADBLOCKS TO GRACE

Those who pursue excellence, discipline, education, and productivity often take them to an extreme that prevents the pursuers from accepting God's grace. Let's take a look at four attitudes that serve as roadblocks to grace.

First, with commitment to excellence, there is often an attitude of intolerance. The pursuit of excellence is noble, but sometimes a commitment to excellence can bring an intolerant attitude. As we strive to do our best, we may begin to judge others for not measuring up to our standards. We forget Paul's admonition to "accept one another, just as Christ also accepted us to the glory of God" (Romans 15:7). Those of us who tend to adopt an intolerant attitude need to pursue Christlikeness in our acceptance of others.

Second, with a lifestyle of discipline, there is often an attitude of impatience and tendency to judge. Though personal discipline is a worthy goal (1 Corinthians 9:24–27), those who achieve a higher level of discipline sometimes gain an ugly companion: impatience toward those who are less disciplined than themselves. If discipline is your strength, praise God for the wonderful asset He has given you! But the undisciplined person whom you struggle to accept may be strong in areas where you are weak. God instructs us to "be patient with everyone" (1 Thessalonians 5:14).

What are your areas of personal weakness where God has demonstrated His tolerance and patience toward you?

_____

_____

_____

_____

How can you demonstrate tolerance and patience toward people who have different gifts and struggles than you do?

_____

_____

_____

_____

Third, with a well-developed education and a taste for the arts and culture, there is often an attitude of elitism. Have you ever felt out of your league culturally or educationally? Like the vagabond character Jack Dawson in the movie *Titanic*, most of us have felt out of place at certain times as we rubbed elbows with people of higher educational attainment and cultural refinement. On the other hand, the more educated and cultured we become, the more we're tempted to look down on those we might consider "below" us, failing to extend them grace—and failing to see our own desperate need for it. When we start feeling superior, we should consider Paul's words to the Corinthians, "What do you have that you did not receive? And if you did receive it, why do you boast as if you had not received it?" (1 Corinthians 4:7). Because everything we have has come to us by God's grace through the people, places, and resources He has provided for us, there's no room for us to boast in our educational or social positions.

Read 1 Corinthians 1:26–31. Given God's perspective on social and educational status, what should our attitude be toward others?

_____

_____

_____

_____

Fourth, with an emphasis on independence and high production, there is often an attitude of pride. Having a can-do attitude certainly has its benefits, but those who model it don't always have an easy time accepting God's grace. Self-made people aren't looking for a handout. They've succeeded, and they're proud of it! But proud people tend to resist God's grace because they believe they have no needs. Recall the words of James: "'GOD IS OPPOSED TO THE PROUD, BUT GIVES GRACE TO THE HUMBLE.' Submit therefore to God. . . . Draw near to God and He will draw near to you" (James 4:6–8).

Intolerance, impatience, elitism, and *pride*—these four roadblocks in the path of God's grace will prevent us from accepting His refreshing provision. For us to be "grace receivers" rather than "grace resisters," these barriers must be removed.

BIBLICAL ACCOUNTS OF GRACE RECEIVERS AND GRACE RESISTERS

Now, let's turn our attention to both positive and negative responses to grace. We'll look at the lives of Moses and Samson in the Old Testament, along with Peter's and Paul's in the New. These men illustrate four invaluable principles for becoming grace receivers.

Moses: An Old Testament Grace Resister

Moses's experience teaches us that *we resist grace when we have not dealt adequately with our guilt.* The son of a Hebrew slave, Moses was adopted by Pharaoh's daughter and raised as royalty. He received the best education that Egypt could offer, was "a man of power in words and deeds" (Acts 7:22), and may have been in line to succeed Pharaoh himself.

When Moses was forty years old, God's prompting led him to turn his attention to delivering his fellow Hebrews from their unjust enslavement. Unfortunately, Moses took matters into his own hands when he murdered an Egyptian who was mistreating a Hebrew slave. Pursued as a murderer by Pharaoh himself, Moses fled to the Sinai desert, where he spent the next forty years working as a shepherd for his father-in-law and wallowing in unresolved shame and guilt.

Yet, despite Moses's feelings of complete inadequacy and uselessness, God had a plan, and it included Moses. In a stunning encounter, God called this washed-up eighty-year-old to free the Hebrews and fulfill God's ancient promises to His people (Exodus 3:1–10). In response to God's call, Moses covered up the guilt of his past with numerous weak excuses for why he shouldn't be the one God would use to deliver His people (Exodus 3:11–4:17).

God knew that Moses had the leadership capacity to lead the Israelites out of bondage. But before Moses could be used by Yahweh, he had to accept His grace. The hesitant leader needed to accept God's forgiveness for his past sins and trust that the Lord would enable him to accomplish the task *in spite of* his past failures and his present weaknesses.

Like Moses, you may be wrestling with unresolved shame and guilt from past choices you've made, and you may be allowing those feelings to prevent God from using you. Are you willing to accept God's forgiveness for your own past failures? If so, tell Him that you choose to accept His grace now, thanking Him for His forgiveness and His willingness to use you as you are.

_____

_____

_____

_____

Samson: An Old Testament Grace Receiver

Samson's life teaches us that *we accept grace when we release our expectations.* Between the time when Joshua led the Israelites into the Promised Land and Saul became Israel's first king, God used a succession of judges to deliver Israel from their oppressors. Among these deliverers was Samson, to whom God had given exceptional physical strength. For twenty years, this mighty warrior led Israel in its fight against foreign oppression (Judges 15:20).

Yet Samson led a double life. Often consumed by his sexual lust (Judges 14–15), he grew careless and complacent. His loose living brought him under the intoxicating influence of a Philistine temptress named Delilah, who conspired to rob Samson of his strength by shaving his head while he slept. By revealing to Delilah the source of his strength, Samson broke his sacred Nazirite vow before God (16:17). When he awoke, the power on which he had always depended had left him. The waiting Philistines bound him, gouged out his eyes, and threw him into prison (16:18–21). Samson was stripped of all his self-sufficiency . . . and his expectations of God. Samson knew he no longer had any right to expect special favors or blessings from Yahweh, because he had broken his promise.

It was at this lowest point of Samson's life, however, that God's grace flowed freely. When the Philistines assembled to celebrate their victory at a pagan temple, they brought in Samson, blind and chained, to mock for entertainment. They tied him between two pillars so they could laugh at him as they reveled. But Samson had the last laugh! As his hair had gradually grown back, so had his strength and his passion for fulfilling his role as vindicator of his people. He acknowledged God as his true source of power and, with no expectations, called on Him for the power to enact one final, spectacular feat.

Read Judges 16:28–30. How did Samson's prayer demonstrate his complete acceptance of God's grace?

_____
_____
_____
_____

How did God answer Samson's prayer?

_____
_____
_____
_____

Peter: A New Testament Grace Resister

Moses resisted God's grace because of his own feelings of guilt and shame. Samson received God's grace by stripping away his own expectations. As we fast forward into the New Testament, we encounter the apostle Peter, who shows us that *we resist grace when our pride is still paramount.*

Peter had many admirable qualities: passionate dedication, boldness, faith, and leadership. But he had an Achilles' heel—his pride. His attitude was, "Just give the job to me, Lord. I can handle it." Time and experience eventually proved to Peter that he was wrong; he *couldn't* handle every situation properly on his own. Yet, at the Last Supper, Peter still brimmed with pride.

Read Matthew 26:30–35. Describe Peter's attitude concerning what Jesus said to the disciples.

_____

_____

_____

_____

In which areas of your life do you tend to think that you can handle things on your own and that you don't really need to depend on God all that much?

_____

_____

_____

Paul: A New Testament Grace Receiver

The last of our four examples is the apostle Paul, who shows us that *we accept grace when we no longer put confidence in the flesh.* Paul learned that when we stop trusting in our own abilities, strengths, and resources, we can receive God's grace. Jesus said, "It is the Spirit who gives life; the flesh profits nothing" (John 6:63). Our flesh—what we bring to the table apart from God—can't produce anything of eternal significance. Only the Holy Spirit can do that.

FLYING AGAINST THE WINDS OF OUR CULTURE

Philip Yancey writes, "Ask people what they must do to get to heaven and most reply, 'Be good.' Jesus's stories contradict that answer. All we must do is cry, 'Help!' God welcomes home anyone who will have him and, in fact, has made the first move already."[1]

In our *Lone Ranger* culture, which encourages us to try to achieve our goals on our own, we pride ourselves on our individual accomplishments and can't stand to share the glory with another. As a result, we face built-in obstacles to receiving God's grace. Our culture is not a culture of grace; it's a culture of merit. Many people fall short of accepting God's gift of salvation because *they forget that they need God.*

Is it possible that you have been rejecting the salvation that God offers you through His Son because you have been unwilling to say to God, "I need You"? God offers each of us the most precious gift He could give: eternal life. It cost Him the life of His own beloved Son. If you would like to make sure today that you have this gift, take a few minutes now to pray. Acknowledge your need, and accept His grace. Place your trust in Jesus Christ, God's Son, who died on the cross for your sins and rose from the dead. Tell your heavenly Father that you want to receive Christ into your life as your personal Savior, to be with Him and enjoy Him forever.

In Philippians 3:4–7, Paul describes what he brought to the table apart from God. According to verses 5 and 6, what qualifications did Paul have on his "religious résumé"?

_____

_____

_____

_____

According to verse 7, how did Paul feel about these qualifications after he received God's grace?

_____
_____
_____
_____

If you were to compose your own "religious résumé" of human strengths and qualifications, what would you include?

_____
_____
_____
_____
_____
_____

How could trusting in your human strengths prevent you from receiving God's grace and being used more fully as His instrument?

_____
_____
_____
_____
_____
_____
_____
_____
_____
_____
_____

GETTING TO THE ROOT

In Philippians 3:8, Paul described all the things he once considered profitable and beneficial as rubbish. The Greek word for "rubbish," *skubalon,* means "refuse, rubbish, leavings, dirt, dung."[2] A note in the The NET Bible (New English Translation) says *skubalon* "would most likely have had a certain shock value for the readers."[3] There is likely no stronger word Paul could have used to express the disdain he had for his personal and religious "qualifications."

Spreading Your Wings

Not putting our confidence in the flesh requires two things.

It takes an admission of our humanity. As long as we expect to do things perfectly and not let any of our weaknesses get in the way, we are putting our confidence in the flesh. But God's grace doesn't operate that way. Second Corinthians 4:7 says, "But we have this treasure in earthen vessels, so that . . . the power will be of God and not from ourselves." Our Father comes to us in our weak humanity and says, "I am willing to use this ordinary, common clay pot to do My will." When we admit that we're imperfect clay pots, we exhibit the power and glory of God's work.

It takes an attitude of humility. It takes a willingness to play second fiddle to God and His work. John the Baptist reflected this attitude when he said of Jesus, "He must increase but I must decrease" (John 3:30). Our hearts must say to God, "I'm not here to make myself somebody. I'm here to point people to You."

When has God used you in spite of your human weaknesses? What does this say about how He may use you in the future?

_____

_____

_____

When we overcome intolerance, impatience, elitism, and pride and replace them with an acceptance of our humanity and an attitude of humility, we become conduits of God's grace. We are then free to accept the grace God offers us—the grace to accept ourselves the way we are, the grace to love others, and the grace to enjoy God and bathe in His unconditional love. Why would anyone not want to receive the grace our heavenly Father, our *Abba*, so freely offers us?

The grace of God says to you and to me,
"I can make last place more significant than first place.
I will use prostitutes to teach others about gratitude.
I will use lepers as examples of cleanliness.
I will take men who persecute the church and make them its pillars.
I will take the dead and give them life.
I will take uneducated fishermen and make them fishers of men."
God's grace does not exist to make us successful.
God's grace exists to point people
to a love like no other love they have ever known.[4]

—MICHAEL YACONELLI

ENDNOTES

Chapter 1

Unless otherwise noted below, all material in this chapter is based on or quoted from "Grace: It's *Really* Amazing!" a sermon by Charles R. Swindoll, September 18, 1988, and chapter 1 of *The Grace Awakening*.

1. H. Freedman and I. Epstein, *Shabbath: Hebrew-English Edition of the Babylonian Talmud* (New York: Soncino Press, 1972), 153.

2. Donald Grey Barnhouse, *Man's Ruin, God's Wrath*, vol. 1 (Grand Rapids, Mich.: Wm. B. Eerdmans Publishing Company, 1952), 72.

3. Augustine, *City of God*, trans. Henry Bettenson (London: Penguin Classics, 1984), 414.

Chapter 2

Unless otherwise noted below, all material in this chapter is based on or quoted from "The Free Gift," a sermon by Charles R. Swindoll, September 25, 1988, and chapter 2 of *The Grace Awakening*.

1. William Ernest Henley, "Invictus," in *The Best Loved Poems of the American People*, selected by Hazel Felleman (Garden City, N.Y.: Doubleday & Company, Inc., 1936), 73.

2. "My Way." Original French words by Giles Thibault; English words by Paul Anka. Copyright for U.S.A. and Canada: Management Agency and Music Publishing (BMI); 1969.

3. John F. Walvoord and Roy B. Zuck, eds., *The Bible Knowledge Commentary* (Wheaton, Ill.: Victor Books, 1985), 44–45.

4. James Russell Lowell, "The Present Crisis," *Bartlett's Familiar Quotations*, 15th and 125th anniversary editions, ed. Emily Morison Beck (Boston: Little, Brown & Co., 1980), 567.

5. Augustus Toplady, *The Works of Augustus Toplady*, B.A. (Glendale, Calif.: Church Press, no date listed), 910. Printed verbatim from the first edition of his works, 1794. London: Printed for J. Chidley, 123, Aldersgate Street, 1837.

6. Dorothea Day, "My Captain," in *The Best Loved Poems of the American People*, 73–74.

7. John Owen, *Sin and Temptation: The Challenges to Personal Godliness*, ed. James M. Houston (Portland, Ore.: Multnomah Press, 1983), 99.

Chapter 3

Unless otherwise noted below, all material in this chapter is based on or quoted from "Isn't Grace Risky?" a sermon by Charles R. Swindoll, October 2, 1988, and chapter 3 of *The Grace Awakening*.

1. Dr. Martyn Lloyd-Jones, *Romans: The New Man, An Exposition of Chapter 6* (Grand Rapids, Mich.: Zondervan Publishing House, 1973), 8–10.

2. Wendell Johnston, "Repentance," in *The Theological Wordbook: The 200 Most Important Theological Terms and Their Relevance for Today* (Nashville: Word Publishing, 2000), 297–98.

3. Philip D. Yancey, *What's So Amazing About Grace?* Copyright © 1997 by Philip D. Yancey (Grand Rapids: The Zondervan Corporation). Used by permission.

4. Edward M. Plass, comp., *What Luther Says: An Anthology* (Saint Louis: Concordia Publishing House, 1972), 614.

Chapter 4

Unless otherwise noted below, all material in this chapter is based on or quoted from "Undeserving, Yet Unconditionally Loved," a sermon by Charles R. Swindoll, October 9, 1988, and chapter 4 of *The Grace Awakening*.

1. Jackie Hudson, "People Grow Better in Grace," *Worldwide Challenge*, April 1988:11, an adaptation from her book *Doubt: A Road to Growth*.

2. John Newton, "Amazing Grace," in *The Hymnal for Worship and Celebration* (Waco, Tex.: Word Music, 1986), no. 202.

Chapter 5

Unless otherwise noted below, all material in this chapter is based on or quoted from "Squaring Off against Legalism," a sermon by Charles R. Swindoll, October 16, 1988, and chapter 5 of *The Grace Awakening*.

1. E. F. Harrison, "Judaizing," in *The International Standard Bible Encyclopedia*, vol. 2, E–J, rev. ed., ed. Geoffrey W. Bromiley, Everett F. Harrison, Roland K. Harrison, and William Sanford LaSor (Grand Rapids, Mich.: William B. Eerdmans Publishing Company, 1982), 1150.

2. Ignatius, *Letter to the Magnesians* 10:3, Michael W. Holmes, ed., *The Apostolic Fathers: Greek Texts and English Translations*, updated ed. (Grand Rapids, Mich.: Baker Books, 1999), 157.

3. Walter Bauer, William F. Arndt, F. Wilbur Gingrich, and Frederick W. Danker, *A Greek-English Lexicon of the New Testament and Other Early Christian Literature*, 2d rev. ed. (Chicago: University of Chicago Press, 1979), 315.

4. Bauer and others, *A Greek-English Lexicon of the New Testament*, 315.

5. Donald K. Campbell, "Galatians," in *The Bible Knowledge Commentary: New*

Testament Edition, ed. John F. Walvoord and Roy B. Zuck (Wheaton, Ill.: Victor Books, 1983), 597; and G. Walter Hansen, *Galatians*, The IVP New Testament Commentary Series, ed. Grand R. Osborne, D. Stuart Briscoe, and Haddon Robinson (Downer's Grove, Ill.: InterVarsity Press, 1994), 82.

6. Bauer and others, *A Greek-English Lexicon of the New Testament*, 302.

7. Jerry Bridges, *Transforming Grace: Living Confidently in God's Unfailing Love* (Colorado Springs, Colo.: NavPress, 1991), 134.

Chapter 6

Unless otherwise noted below, all material in this chapter is based on or quoted from "Emancipated? Then Live Like It!" a sermon by Charles R. Swindoll, October 23, 1988, and chapter 6 of *The Grace Awakening*.

1. Shelby Foote, *The Civil War: Red River to Appomattox* (New York: Random House, 1974), 1045.

2. John Stott, *Romans: God's Good News for the World* (Downers Grove, Ill.: InterVarsity Press, 1994), 180.

Chapter 7

Unless otherwise noted below, all material in this chapter is based on or quoted from "Guiding Others to Freedom," a sermon by Charles R. Swindoll, October 30, 1988, and chapter 7 of *The Grace Awakening*.

1. David K. Lowery, "1 Corinthians," in John F. Walvoord and Roy B. Zuck, eds., *The Bible Knowledge Commentary, New Testament* (Wheaton, Ill.: Victor Books, 1983), 520.

2. William Barclay, *The Daily Study Bible, The Letter to the Romans* (Philadelphia: The Westminster Press, 1975), 90–91.

Chapter 8

Unless otherwise noted below, all material is based on or quoted from "The Grace to Let Others Be," a sermon by Charles R. Swindoll, November 6, 1988, and chapter 8 of *The Grace Awakening*.

1. Viktor Frankl, *Man's Search for Meaning* (New York: Washington Square Press, Pocket Books, 1985), 86-87. Used by permission of Beacon Press.

2. Philip D. Yancey, *What's So Amazing About Grace?* Copyright © 1997 by Philip D. Yancey (Grand Rapids: The Zondervan Corporation). Used by permission.

Chapter 9

Unless otherwise noted below, all material in this chapter is based on or quoted from "Graciously Disagreeing and Pressing On," a sermon by Charles R. Swindoll, November 13, 1988, and chapter 9 of *The Grace Awakening*.

1. Walter Bauer, William F. Arndt, F. Wilbur Gingrich, and Frederick W. Danker, *A Greek-English Lexicon of the New Testament and Other Early Christian Literature*, 2d rev. ed. (Chicago: University of Chicago Press, 1979), 102.

2. Bauer and others, *A Greek-English Lexicon of the New Testament*, 126.

3. *Merriam-Webster's Collegiate Dictionary*, 10th ed., see "apostasy."

4. Bauer and others, *A Greek-English Lexicon of the New Testament*, 629; *Merriam-Webster's Collegiate Dictionary*, 10th ed., see "paroxysm."

5. J. I. Packer, "Orthodoxy," in *The Concise Evangelical Dictionary of Theology*, ed. Walter A. Elwell, abridged by Peter Toon (Grand Rapids: Baker Book House, 1991), 364.

6. C. S. Lewis in an unpublished letter to Dom Bede Griffiths, O.S.B. (c. 1933), quoted in Walter Hooper, "Preface," in C. S. Lewis, *Christian Reflections*, ed. Walter Hooper (Grand Rapids, Mich.: William B. Eerdmans Publishing Company, 1967), vii.

Chapter 10

Unless otherwise noted below, all material in this chapter is based on or quoted from "Grace: Up Close and Personal," a sermon by Charles R. Swindoll, November 20, 1988, and chapter 10 of *The Grace Awakening*.

1. John Bunyan, *The Pilgrim's Progress: From This World to That Which Is to Come* (Uhrichsville, Ohio: Barbour Publishing, 1993), 17.

2. *Merriam-Webster's Collegiate Dictionary*, 10th ed., see "humanism."

3. John Newton, "Amazing Grace," in *The Hymnal for Worship and Celebration* (Waco, Tex.: Word Music, 1986), no. 202.

4. C. S. Lewis, *Mere Christianity*. Copyright © C. S. Lewis Pte. Ltd. 1942, 1943, 1944, 1952. Extract reprinted by permission.

Chapter 11

Unless otherwise noted below, all material in this chapter is based on or quoted from "Are You *Really* a Minister of Grace?" a sermon by Charles R. Swindoll, November 27, 1988, and chapter 11 of *The Grace Awakening*.

1. A. Skevington Wood, "Ephesians," in *The Expositor's Bible Commentary*, ed., Frank E. Gaebelein and J. D. Douglas, vol. 11, *Ephesians–Philemon* (Grand Rapids, Mich.: Zondervan Publishing House, 1978), 42; *Nelson's Illustrated Bible Dictionary*, ed. Herbert Lockyer, Sr. (Nashville: Thomas Nelson, 1986), see "capstone," "cornerstone," and "foundation."

2. Adapted from Bruce Wilkinson and Kenneth Boa, *Talk Thru the Old Testament*, vol. 1 of *Talk Thru the Bible* (Nashville: Thomas Nelson, 1983), 283–84.

3. F. Duane Lindsey, "Zechariah" in *The Bible Knowledge Commentary, Old Testament*, ed. John F. Walvoord and Roy B. Zuck (Wheaton, Ill.: Victor Books, SP Publications, 1985), 1555.

4. Theodore Laetsch, *Bible Commentary: The Minor Prophets* (St. Louis, Mo: Concordia Publishing House, 1970), 428.

5. George Duffield, Jr., "Stand Up, Stand Up for Jesus," in *The Hymnal for Worship and Celebration* (Waco, Tex.: Word Music, 1986), no. 477.

Chapter 12

Unless otherwise noted below, all material in this chapter is based on or quoted from "A Marriage Oiled by Grace," a sermon by Charles R. Swindoll, December 4, 1988, and chapter 12 of *The Grace Awakening*.

1. Eugene H. Peterson, *Run with the Horses: The Quest for Life at Its Best* (Downers Grove, Ill.: InterVarsity Press, 1983), 159–60.

2. Leonhard Goppelt, *A Commentary on 1 Peter*, ed. Ferdinand Hahn, trans. John E. Alsup (Grand Rapids, Mich.: William B. Eerdmans Publishing Company, 1993), 159.

3. Willard F. Harley, Jr., *His Needs, Her Needs* (Old Tappan, N.J.: Fleming H. Revell Company, 1986), 10.

4. Martin Luther, "The Estate of Marriage," in *Luther's Works*, vol. 45, *The Christian in Society II*, ed. Walther I. Brandt and Helmut T. Lehmann (Philadelphia: Muhlenberg, 1962), 42.

Chapter 13

Unless otherwise noted below, all material in this chapter is based on or quoted from "The Charming Joy of Grace Giving," a sermon by Charles R. Swindoll, December 11, 1988, and chapter 13 of *The Grace Awakening*.

1. From a lecture by Ronald W. Blue, president of Christian Financial Professionals Network (CFPN), 5605 Glenridge Drive, Suite 845, Atlanta, Georgia 30342. (www.cfpn.org) Used by permission.

2. *Merriam-Webster's Collegiate Dictionary*, 10th ed., see "hilarious" and "hilarity."

3. Walter Bauer, William F. Arndt, F. Wilbur Gingrich, and Frederick W. Danker, *A Greek-English Lexicon of the New Testament and Other Early Christian Literature*, 2d rev. ed. (Chicago: University of Chicago Press, 1979), 375.

4. Calvin Miller, "The Gift of Giving," Moody Monthly (December 1988): 24.

Chapter 14

Unless otherwise noted below, all material in this chapter is based on or quoted from "Grace: It's *Really* Accepting!" a sermon by Charles R. Swindoll, December 18, 1988, and chapter 14 of *The Grace Awakening*.

1. Philip D. Yancey, *What's So Amazing About Grace?* Copyright © 1997 by Philip D. Yancey (Grand Rapids: The Zondervan Corporation). Used by permission.

2. Walter Bauer, William F. Arndt, F. Wilbur Gingrich, and Frederick W. Danker, *A Greek-English Lexicon of the New Testament and Other Early Christian Literature*, 2d rev. ed. (Chicago: University of Chicago Press, 1979), 758.

3. The NET Bible, New English Translation, (Dallas: Biblical Studies Press, 1998), 623, note 13.

4. Michael Yaconelli, *Dangerous Wonder: The Adventure of Childlike Faith* (Colorado Springs, Colo.: NavPress, 1998), 130.

BOOKS FOR PROBING FURTHER

W E HOPE YOUR TIME SPENT in *The Grace Awakening Workbook* has given you the truths you need to fly free. As you say no to legalistic standards and yes to God's love, you'll truly soar.

May you be free to follow God out of desire rather than guilt, and may you free others to do the same. Use the following list of books to discover more about God's truly amazing and accepting grace!

Bridges, Jerry. *Transforming Grace: Living Confidently in God's Unfailing Love.* Colorado Springs, Colo.: NavPress, 1993.

Chafer, Lewis Sperry. *Grace: An Exposition of God's Marvelous Gift.* Grand Rapids, Mich.: Kregel Publications, 1995.

Crabb, Larry. *The Pressure's Off.* Colorado Springs, Colo.:Waterbrook Press, 2002.

Lloyd-Jones, D. Martyn. *Romans: The New Man: Exposition of Chapter 6.* Grand Rapids, Mich.: Zondervan Publishing House, 1979.

Lucado, Max. *Grace for the Moment*. Nashville, Tenn.: J. Countryman Books., 2000.

Lucado, Max. *In the Grip of Grace*. Nashville, Tenn.: Word Publishing, 1996.

Manning, Brennan. *Abba's Child: The Cry of the Heart for Intimate Belonging*. Colorado Springs., Colo.: Navpress, 2002.

Manning, Brennan. *The Ragamuffin Gospel*. Sisters: Ore.: Multnomah Publishers Inc., 2000.

Mason, Mike. *The Mystery of Marriage: Meditations on the Miracle*. Sisters: Ore.: Multnomah Publishers Inc., 2001.

McVey, Steve. *Grace Walk*. Eugene, Ore.: Harvest House Publishers Inc., 1995.

Seamands, David. *Healing Grace: Finding a Freedom from the Performance Trap*. Indianapolis, Ind.: Life and Light Communications, 1999.

Stedman, Ray C. *Authentic Christianity: The Classic Bestseller on Living the Life of Faith With Integrity*. Nashville, Tenn.: Thomas Nelson, 1996.

Smedes, Lewis B. *Forgive and Forget: Healing the Hurts We Don't Deserve*. New York, N.Y.: Pocket Books, 1990.

Smedes, Lewis B. *Shame and Grace*. New York, N.Y.: HarperCollins, 1994.

Stott, John. R. W. *The Message of Romans*. Downers Grove, Ill.: Intervarsity Press, 2001.

Tournier, Paul. *Guilt and Grace: A Psychological Study*. New York, N.Y.: HarperCollins, 1982.

Vanvonderen, Jeff. *Families Where Grace Is in Place*. Minneapolis, Minn.: Bethany House Publishers, 1992.

Vanvonderen, Jeff. *Tired of Trying to Measure Up*. Minneapolis, Minn.: Bethany House Publishers, 1989.

Yaconelli, Michael. *Messy Spirituality*. Grand Rapids, Mich.: Zondervan Publishing House, 2002.

Yancey, Phillip. *What's So Amazing About Grace?* Grand Rapids: Mich.: Zondervan Publishing House, 1997.